D0436059

justification by success

J. Stanley Glen

WITHDRAWN

justification by success

THE INVISIBLE CAPTIVITY of THE CHURCH

JOHN KNOX PRESS
ATLANTA

HIEBERT LIBRARY
Pacific College - M. B. Seminary
Fresno, Calif. 93702

14823

Unless otherwise noted, Scripture quotations are from the Revised Standard Version Bible, copyright 1946, 1952, and © 1971 by the Division of Christian Education, National Council of the Churches of Christ in the U.S.A. and used by permission.

Library of Congress Cataloging in Publication Data
Glen, John Stanley, 1907–
  Justification by success.

  Includes bibliographical references.
  1. Christianity—20th century. I. Title.
BR121.2.G53   209'.04   78–52446
ISBN 0–8042–0835–2

Copyright © 1979 John Knox Press
Printed in the United States of America

contents

preface

This study developed slowly out of increasing curiosity about the nature, complexity, and acceleration of change which is virtually global in its scope. At the same time the historically unprecedented character of such change (which affected virtually all sectors of society, including government, business, industry, education, entertainment, family life, and religion) added to the curiosity. All of this began to lead more and more to the conviction that it was a theological problem of the first order of magnitude, which by its very nature probably pertained to the Judeo-Christian religion more seriously than to any other religion.

A parallel conviction began to emerge that such change was itself the communication of an ideology which was inherent in science, technology, and technique—particularly in the latter two. As such it was the ideology which was built into advanced industrial society objectively and common to Neo-Capitalism, Communism, Socialism, Fascism, and other comparable social orders. Indeed, it qualified under the category of an invisible religion as defined by sociologist Thomas Luckmann.

Further curiosity began to develop as a number of affinities were recognized between this ideology or invisible religion on the one hand and the Judeo-Christian religion on the other. How to explain these affinities posed a dilemma which Judeo-Christian theology seemed not as yet to have recognized, nor for which to have provided any answer. Beyond this, however, it seemed that any answer would require action, perhaps a rather radical form of action such as a new reformation. The necessity of such an answer is emphasized in the section on "the captivity of the church" in chapter six. This implies the seriousness of the need for liberation at the very heart of the Judeo-Christian religion.

At this point it is appropriate to say that the spontaneous encouragement given me by the Canadian Council of Churches to publish this volume has been a real source of inspiration and helpfulness, for which it is impossible to express adequate appreciation. This encouragement came in response to an address given to the Council in October, 1976, on "the captivity of the church" which is part of this volume. It also arose out of the discussion following the address, which ranged over most of the major themes of the previous chapters.

My gratitude is extended to Mrs. James Carruthers whose assistance in typing the manuscript was indispensible, especially in view of her expertise as secretary to me while I was Principal of Knox College, Toronto, Canada. A deep, heartfelt tribute to my wife Winifred is most appropriate also because of the encouragement given me over the years of study required to produce this volume, her association with me on sabbatical leave in New College, University of Edinburgh, where part of the research was done, and the inspiration of her faith and role in my life.

1.
the invisible religion

Unlike those civilizations which have remained relatively static and stable, modern civilization has been characterized by unusual social change and a comparable instability. From the fourteenth through the seventeenth into the nineteenth century, when industrialism with its factory system and urbanization had been rather extensively developed, especially in Britain, the tempo of social change steadily increased. The tempo varied from one region to another just as the pattern varied, as reflected in industrial, urban, and colonial expansion and accompanying social problems. In certain critical periods the resultant tension and dislocation contributed to conditions which at times erupted into revolution and warfare. In recent history, including the latter part of the nineteenth and the early twentieth centuries and especially since the Second World War, this unusual social change and its accompanying instability has reached unprecedented proportions.

The result has been that modern civilization has put increasing pressure upon everything that signifies the unchangeable, such as the eternal, the essential, and the traditional. In recent times it has tended to obscure and call these into question more than ever before. As a result the old regimes, styles, and laws, as well as the old religions, philosophies, and values, have either persisted on the defensive or lost their substance and eventually disappeared. In an almost total, comprehensive environment of change in which increasing pressure comes from every direction, any crucial concept of permanence is difficult to maintain. This means that religious faith centered on the eternal, unchangeable character of God—the One who is the same yesterday, today, and forever—is especially vulnerable. It means that any philosophy which gives essence of being and objective value the connotation of permanence is similarly vulnerable. In practice it means the erosion of the historical and moral values by which the order of any society is best maintained.

The recognition of the unusual social change which characterizes modern civilization, especially in its advanced industrial form, leads to an axiomatic observation. Such change is a product of unusual power and reflects the many sources and varieties of power and their collective impact. No other civilization ever developed such power, especially the ever-increasing specialized forms of power which science and technology along with money and organization have been able to produce. No other civilization ever developed such an obsession for power, which as such has even transcended the most lurid historical examples of a Promethean lust for power. If anything, the process has been circular. The more power that has been procured, the more the desire for power has expanded, especially the fascination with the ever-increasing specialized forms of power. At the same time the specialized forms have tended to integrate and to increase exponentially and to stimulate the desire for power and particularly the fascination with it. As a result of such a circular process, the temptation has emerged more than ever of seeing in the unprecedented power of modern civilization the potentiality of the infinite.

As often as the pursuit of power has yielded to this temptation, power has become an end in itself and for practical purposes the equivalent of deity. The hidden, unacknowledged confidence has been that such power signifies the ultimate and therefore the objective which man should glorify and enjoy as the chief end of life. This has been implied in the total manner in which individuals and corporate bodies have dedicated themselves to various kinds of interrelated power—money, profits, growth and expansion, science and technology, bureaucracy and armaments. In such total dedication to these various kinds of power, which though many are yet one in their integrated achievement, power is considered in effect the one and only god which gives tangible and practical results. Like the God of the Bible who is so characteristically dynamic, this god in its own way is similarly dynamic. It is not static and abstract but highly operative here and now as a god which acts. It is readily available and near at hand and full of hope and promise.

But beyond the stage of possessing power as an end in itself, there is a pinnacle of power which the possessor can reach, either as an individual or as a corporate body which signifies a degree of autonomy that is virtually absolute. At this point the possessor is able to set prices, determine profits, make laws directly or indirectly as well as policies and practices, create values styles and practices, define the good, and make truth in what is described as "messages" (ads) and news, each of which is selected by norms that sell. By various means the same possessor can even make history by creating events or pseudo-events which will be recorded. At this pinnacle of power the possessor either as an individual or corporate body is virtually the incarnation of power and therefore the manifestation ("revelation") of the sovereignty of the power god in particularized form.

The problem, however, is that such a pinnacle of power is difficult to achieve and more difficult to maintain. This is because social change as a product of power always poses a threat to power. Such power is not eternal and unchangeable and is therefore always exposed to competition and danger in addition to natural contingency. Its advantage is always being eroded and undermined, however imperious it may appear to be. Its deity is always being threatened by deities of a similar kind. Consequently, one of the most frequent solutions of the problem has been aggression and expansion which overcome competitive deities and secure a monopoly over them. They are either conquered, bankrupted, or absorbed, and their threat eliminated. For this reason such monopolism provides the nearest equivalent of the eternal and the unchangeable. It provides the nearest equivalent of the omnipotence of the power god, especially as it is extended to a national dimension and more especially to a multi-national dimension.

But, whatever the extent, the implicit faith of monopolism involves a dedication to the power god as the one god beside which there is no other or at least should be no other gods (cf. Deuteronomy 4:35; Isaiah 45:5). This means that the monopolism of the power god is its equivalent of *monotheism.* By its faith in aggressive action, it hopes to achieve more and more monopoly until in the end it has triumphed over all its competitors and emerged as the one and only god. Its aggressive action is its equivalent of missionary endeavor, by which it hopes to prove its competitors weak and for this reason false.

Out of these various reflections on unusual power as the source of unusual social change arises another axiomatic observation. It indicates one of the most important reasons why such power succeeds in acquiring more or less of a monopolistic domination in one form or another over vast sectors of society and of the world. It is the recognition that unusual power invariably presupposes unusual secrecy as one of the most effective means of achieving such an objective. In a variety of ways such power operates anonymously under a cover of silence without being advertised or publicized in the news. This characterizes not only police and military operations but business, industrial, financial and political operations. As a simple illustration, a merchant does not reveal the wholesale price of his goods to his customers. They have no way of knowing his markup. This is considered private and therefore secret. As private enterprise it is therefore secret enterprise. Beyond this simple example the world of corporate business, of industrial and financial enterprise, operates on the same principle of secrecy. In view of the size and complexity of such a world, its operations amount to a major dimension of secrecy. Crucial maneuvers often have their definitive setting in a back room with only a few trusted associates and protected by the most guarded forms of communication. The movements of top personnel are kept secret even from many of those in the higher echelons of the same organization. Their telephone numbers are unlisted and their names kept as private as possible. They avoid any visible participation in politics. The task of contacting them personally involves the penetration of a succession of bureaucratic facades with ample validation of the identity and purpose of the patron.

The same can be said of political operations. Private conversations with representatives of vested interests take precedence over the privacy of party caucuses and closed committee meetings in what often leads to secret commitments. The increasing power of the executive branch of government facilitates these consultations, which are often described as privileged in the national interest. No matter what form of government may be in power, even the most democratic, this unusual secrecy prevails with only selected items being released to the press. The open debate of legislative assemblies and the staged election issues only reveal a mere fraction of the vast realm of secrecy below the surface. In effect the daily news is scarcely news at all because it is chosen and packaged for sale and is not permitted to endanger the hidden power that promotes it.

A similar observation can be made of the whole of society, particularly of an *urbanized, mass society* in which the stranger is by definition a secret. The next door "neighbor" in the same block or apartment is virtually anonymous. Caution is exercised in sharing information with him. Even in the same social circle a similar caution is exercised which is often concealed under "free and easy" chatter on non-essential items. The average individual has to protect his limited resources and possessions by such secrecy. He has few if any trusted relatives and friends with whom he can be open on private matters. In this respect his meager power has to be protected by secrecy, which as such is a form of security.

In view of these various aspects of the secrecy of power in every sector of advanced industrial, urbanized, mass society, the axiomatic observation on secrecy as essential to power should be further elaborated. Following the insight of a distinguished authority on the origins of totalitarianism, it can be said that, in any advanced industrial society, "real power begins where secrecy begins" and the more visible the authority the less power it has.[1] This insight pertains to more than totalitarian states. It pertains to any highly developed industrial society with its vast cities and its bureaucratic technological complexity.

Consequently, when power is sought as an end in itself, and thus becomes the equivalent of deity, its essential operation and authority are characterized by a hiddenness which bears an analogy to the biblical God. This is the hiddenness which is indicated by the theological term "deus absconditus," used to indicate that the revelation of the biblical God is always indirect and clothed in mystery. As applied to the domain of the power god, it means that the domain of such a god, like that of the secret kingdom (sovereignty) of the unseen God of biblical faith, involves its own peculiar secret. For this reason the secret of either deity and that of either domain can be accommodated to the other if the line (transcendent) between them is blurred and each regarded more or less as a form of the other. If the primary dedication is to the power god this can mean that the one Almighty God (omnipotent) of biblical faith can be easily used to conceal, promote, and legitimize the power god. The monotheism of the former can be easily used to vindicate the monopolism of the latter.

As another axiomatic observation which supplements the previous one, it can be said that the secrecy of power is facilitated by the unprecedented complexity of contemporary society, particularly in its advanced industrial form. The total, comprehensive nature of the complexity is a product of sophisticated technology and the proliferation of technique in every area of human life. In its organizational form the complexity is illustrated by the prevalence of bureaucracy, which in turn prevents clarity of understanding of what is actually happening. Thousands upon thousands of minute administrative decisions are made behind a variety of facades which in their cumulative effect have a major impact upon society. Countless interlocking systems, each requiring specialized personnel, tend to bind the whole of society together in what develops into an increasingly totalitarian form of integration. As the individual adapts to it all, he is "plugged into" a particular system and in different ways into the interlocking systems not only physically but psychologically. Accompanying the bureaucracy and the interlocking systems is a proliferation of technique which has an even greater effect upon him. Its complexity is subtler, more subliminal, and as a result facilitates the secrecy of power to a greater degree. The commonest illustrations are propaganda, advertising, and public relations, which are part of a vast environmental network of managerial manipulation based upon the behavioral sciences.[2] It comprehends almost every aspect of human life and for this reason is generally accepted as normal by the average individual. Associated with all of these forms of complexity are comparable forms of legal complexity, as legislation spawns new regulations to match the development of technology and technique. This means that society is further enveloped with a proliferation of legal minutiae which often surpasses the comprehension of the best legal minds.

As a result the individual is incapable of find his way through the total complexity which comprehends his life. He has little if any insight into it as a whole and is unable to identify the priorities which are built into it or the vested interests which are served by it. As a citizen he is largely disenfranchised. He cannot vote intelligently. He cannot evaluate the proposals of political parties. His situation is in sharp contrast to that presupposed by the original democratic tradition in which he had a rather comprehensive knowledge of a relatively simple society or at least of a considerable segment of it. The same is true of his situation in every other area—business, industry, finance, government, education, and organized religion as each develops more specialized bureaucracy and domination by central agencies. He is disenfranchised by complexity[3] and yet he is known by the power hidden within the complexity. He is known by its statisticians, accountants, auditors, lawyers, and record keepers who constitute an intelligence core by which the individual is known by such power. Since they are assisted by all the devices of advanced technology for this purpose, such as computers, memory banks, and electronic surveillance, he is known by what may be described as *cybernetic omniscience*. If he has any doubt of being known in this manner by the power god, he need only consider the immediate evidence of his own experience. He has more forms to complete, reports to make, licences to procure, cards to carry, and statistics to provide than in any other period in history.

Again there is a peculiar analogy to the omniscience of the God of the Bible. To describe his situation in biblical terms, he is known of the power god yet he himself does not know such a god directly as an object of experience and thought. He is grasped by the god, yet without him being able to grasp the god in a comparable manner. To use the words of Psalm 139:1, the power god "has searched and known" him, but as stated in verse 4 he himself cannot attain such knowledge. He cannot know himself as the power god knows him. Or to use a closer analogy, the words of Galatians 4:9 will suffice, in which Paul puts the emphasis upon being "known by

God" as the typical knowledge of God rather than direct knowledge as if God were an "object" of human comprehension. In other
words the biblical God is active, assumes the initiative, and knows
him and understands all his ways (cf. Psalm 139:1—6). But he himself
is relatively passive and can only wonder at the mystery of it all.
Thus there is a certain if not a peculiar analogy with the knowledge
which the power god has of the individual. The latter is relatively
passive and can only wonder at it all. As a result he is conditioned
to be a servant of the word of the power god and therefore to do
what he is told to do by its cybernetic omniscience.

At this stage another axiomatic observation must be made. This
will show how the secrecy of power, its drive towards monopolism,
and its practical equivalent of omniscience are further promoted.
This is its emphasis upon a *positive public image.* Historically speaking this has always been a strategy of the powerful in order to
secure the loyalty of the public. Color, style, and ceremony have
served the powerful in providing an attractive image with which the
public could identify. But in any advanced industrial society the
positive public image is further promoted by the amazing achievements of the great variety of machines typical of the mechanical age
and a similar variety of facilities typical of the electrical age. In
general this means the positive impression upon the public mind of
mass production, skills, and services along with the marvels of communication, transportation, and cybernation. As a result the majority
of people have been greatly impressed, their expectations greatly
enlarged, and their impression of the power behind it all heightened
to a new level of the positive. The image of such power with all its
research and development, invention and innovation, and its contribution to a rising standard of living has been more favorable than
ever before. As a result the majority of the public identify more
closely with such power and its creativity. In effect they bear witness
to the power god as a creator god. For this reason they more
readily become its obedient servants and give thanks for all its
wonderful works (compare Psalm 93:3; Psalm 145:4—5).

As the mechanical age gave way to the electrical age, popular
expectations expanded at times to incredible proportions. This was
more evident in the immediate past, particularly in the late sixties
when the positive impact of an unprecedented gross national prod-

uct approaching one trillion dollars in America was increasingly recognized. As a result positive speculation on the shape of the future sharply increased. A rather widely held opinion contended that automated abundance would greatly reduce the necessity of work or at least the more rigorous forms of it. Some indulged in the vision of an era in which the individual would be paid not to work in what amounted to a life of leizure. This signified a technological equivalent of salvation by grace alone in which success as salvation would be entirely gratuitous. Such an extravagant vision of abundance bore a striking resemblance to those ancient biblical and extra-biblical apocalyptic visions of the millenium in which a similar degree of abundance was one of the principal characteristics.[4]

Some speculated that such an era of automated abundance would provide the freedom by which the individual could realize his creative potential more than ever before. Some saw it as improving his ethical life inasmuch as rivalry and competition would be greatly reduced.[5] Others saw the new technology as capable of constructing cities of apocalyptic glory and splendor—mile-high cities, satellite cities orbiting the earth, domed as well as underground cities,[6] each serving a liberated population living a life of leisure and fulfilment solely by the grace of the same automated abundance. The ultimate confidence which tended to emerge was that man could have any kind of world he liked. He could shape the future according to his design. Indeed, he could invent the future.[7] It was as if the millenium were now under new management and the secular city were a redesigned and improved model of the biblical vision of the new Jerusalem. As a result, scarcely anything was as effective for the concealment and promotion of power as these extravagant speculations. The positive image had reached a new level of grandeur. The inherent correlation of power with glory had been achieved.

There was, however, a threshold at which the positive was transformed into the negative. As a further axiomatic observation this was the threshold at which the *adulation* of power was transformed into alienation. To this point power and social change had a positive image, but beyond this point they acquired a negative image. They generated criticism, opposition, disillusionment, disorientation, and feelings of insignificance and powerlessness which

deepened into apathy and normlessness. At times this peculiar combination of alienation exploded into violence and serious social
strife. This was partly because of the repressive, exploitative character of power and social change and partly because of deterioration
of quality, acceleration of tempo, and adverse effects upon people
and the environment. The basic reason was that man's increasing
power over nature had become to a large extent the increasing
power of some men over other men with nature as their instrument.[8]

The exercise of such power was not only intentional but multi-
consequential, to which power for all its emphasis on secrecy has
always been surprisingly blind. Indeed, the irony of the concern for
secrecy by the powerful throughout history has always been that
they are blinded by the power which they pursue. As an ironical form
of secrecy this blindness prevents them from seeing the negative
consequences of their power, both upon individuals and society and
upon the environment. They cannot see their sin, which for this
reason remains invisible to them. Or, more exactly expressed, they
prefer to repress and determine not to see it. This at once suggests
that the will to power is always to a significant extent the will to
blindness.

As a result of this threshold between the positive and the negative, there are two main classes in modern civilization, especially in
its advanced industrial form. These may be designated by a variety
of synonyms: the overclass and the underclass, the successful and
the unsuccessful, the winners and the losers, the insiders and the
outsiders.[9] In the context of dedication to the power god they may
be designated as the saved and the unsaved, the elect and the
damned. In practice the distinction between them cannot be clearly
drawn. This is because it is only partially a class distinction, which
in turn means that the alienation which defines the distinction may
also enter the upper and middle levels of the class structure even
though it more commonly enters the lower levels. A rich and privileged member of the upper class, for example, may become alienated by indulgence and become a dropout and therefore a loser.
A careerist of the middle class may become alienated by the "rat
race" and become a dissident and in this respect a less obvious kind
of loser.

Thus among the losers and therefore among the unsaved are not only the poor, the powerless, the deprived, and the insignificant elements in society commonly associated with the lower classes, but a variety of others. The latter include those at all levels of society who for a combination of reasons have become alienated against it. They may have become weary of the implosive imagery, the manipulative advertising, the artificial supermarket mentality, the highrise imprisonment, the relentless urban sprawl, the loss of community and family life, the pollution of air and water, the depletion of natural resources, the loss of arable land, and the whole glossy plastic depersonalizing effect of the so-called advanced industrial society. In their own way they see the sin which remains invisible to the devotees of power.

As contributing factors to this invisible sin and the alienation of the unsaved, science, technology, and technique as instruments in the hands of the devotees of the power god have played a most conspicuous role. Just as they contributed to the mechanical age and its transition into the electrical age, so they contributed to the nuclear age and its transition into the space age. Their amazing production of dangerous knowledge belied all previous tradition that knowledge was necessarily good and beneficial. Their provision of the means of nuclear, chemical, and bacteriological warfare which could virtually wipe out the whole human race, if not all forms of life, was the extreme opposite of the positive as represented in automated abundance and fantasies of cities of unprecedented glory and splendor. As a negative form of social change, the possibility of such warfare made the biblical conception of hell seem antiquated and Armageddon obsolete. If the millenium were under new management, there was as much or more evidence that hell was under new management, particularly when the solid evidence of death camps, torture chambers, and brainwashing in various parts of the modern world were taken into consideration. If all of this signified that man was inventing his future, it seemed more probable that he was inviting his end. As the eschatology of the worship of power it seemed like his technological termination. The dominion given him over the earth according to biblical testimony (Psalm 8:6–8) had been transposed by him into an unprecedented domination out of an equally unprecedented dedication to the power god. The enigmatic question which emerged out of this eschatological negative was obvious. Why had man become so destructive? Why had he become such a mass killer (thinking in terms of mega-deaths) in sharp contrast to the other beasts of the earth? Why was he in effect so dedicated to death? Was this the goal to which all his greedy quest for power would finally lead him and his advanced industrial society? Was this the real secret hidden within the secret of power to which he was blind or willfully blind—namely, a pro-found necrophilia—as if the only alternatives were "victory" (power) or death?

This strange threshold between the positive and the negative so characteristic of advanced industrial society was illustrated histori-cally by the outbreak of the First World War in 1914. As the turning point or axial date between what had been so generally positive throughout the nineteenth century, this date signified a kind of historical threshhold which divided one era from another and re-vealed the hidden dilemma of developing power in Western Civili-zation.

From August 1914 forward, man's power over the natural and social order manifested increasingly dangerous and destructive forms which could ultimately become self-defeating and suicidal. Few, even of the most discerning minds, had foreseen the possibility of negative social change as evidenced in war of such proportions and savagery. Few had foreseen the significance of such war as the beginning of a convulsive period of over thirty years (1914–1945) including the Second World War, all of which was unprecedented in world history. None had foreseen the destructive potential of the atom and hydrogen bombs and intercontinental ballistic missiles which symbolized the new dimension of warfare which emerged in the decades following the Second World War.

The momentum of progress prior to 1914 and high levels of culture, scholarship, and gentility had so infused the social con-sciousness that the hidden operations of the great sources of power were generally undetected. But when war of such proportions and savagery broke out, followed by revolutions and the emergence of various forms of unprecedented totalitarianism such as Communism, Fascism, and Nazism with all the startling revelations of their ruth-lessness, it was realized that such negative social change was an eruption from the hidden depths of the social unconscious. In some strange way barbarism was a hidden component of progress and facilitated by the power of the positive.

At the same time the dilemma was deepened by the extent to which Christians slaughtered Christians and churches arrayed themselves against each other, presumably praying to the same God of love for victory over the other. Through it all they were motivated by the primacy of faith in their flags and the glory of sacrifice on the battlefield symbolized by the militarized sword-embossed cross of Christ. The so-called "lesser calvaries" of those who paid the supreme sacrifice was one of several influences which cast the crucified Christ in the role of one whose sacrifice sanctioned the sacrifice of other Christians (the enemies) by means of bayonets, machine guns, bombs, planes, and tanks. At this point certain crucial questions emerged: Was this only a magnified version of what happens in peacetime among Christians who are in competition with one another in business, politics, and international affairs? Why had the love and compassion so central to the message of the New Testament become so peripheral? Why on the other hand had the flag become so central and sacred? What had happened to Christ, the original "good news" (gospel), the nineteenth century missionary concern to win the world for Christ? Was this the way to win the world for him? What had really happened to the Christian faith? Indeed, the evidence strongly indicated that it was in captivity to nationalism and to the hidden sources of power which exploited nationalism.

Such a dilemma in which barbarism is not only a hidden component of national progress but of organized Christianity itself concerns what may be called the crisis of modernity. Broadly speaking, it concerns the split between the positive and the negative which so deeply divides and confuses contemporary civilization. A number of interrelated examples will at least suggest the nature of the dilemma which is virtually indefinable.

On the one hand there is scientific and technological knowledge which, along with its economic and human benefits, has been unprecedented to the point of wonder and millenial awe. On the other hand, the same knowledge includes the dangerous and the destructive to the point of hellish horror and new dimensions of the demonic. What so quickly magnified the dilemma was the knowl-

edge explosion in science, technology, and technique which oc-
curred during the three decades following the Second World War.
During this thirty-year period, colleges, universities, and institutes
increased as much or more than they had in all areas of learning
during the previous eight hundred years.[10]

Closely related to the explosion of knowledge is an emphasis
on economic growth by corporations, which have expanded to an
unprecedented extent in a multi-national dimension. Their drive for
economic growth is to a surprising extent a repetitious "more, more,
more" as the answer to every basic human problem, and this in the
name of freedom. On the other hand, the serious depletion of
natural resources by such greed and prodigality in the interests of
power and a so-called higher standard of living is compounded by
the population explosion, particularly in the "Third World." Along
with the pollution of the environment and the loss or misuse of arable
land, the problem of feeding the world's hungry masses is becoming
acute. The number of poor, hungry, and starving people is steadily
multiplying. As a result serious questions emerge. Where will it all
end? Will it eventually mean a new economic asceticism in order to
survive? Will it go even further and end in what may be called an
ecological Armageddon?

As a final example of the split between the positive and the
negative, there is on the one hand the trend towards an increasingly
integrated, interdependent world, the logic of which leads in the
direction of some kind of multi-national, if not global, totalitarianism.
This is primarily a technological and global totalitarianism hidden
beneath the surface of national and international affairs. But given
the appropriate time and circumstances, it could emerge as a form
of political totalitarianism.

On the other hand, in reaction against the promotion of an
integrated, interdependent world by corporate power, there is a
trend toward greater pluralism. New nations are emerging, the
majority of which are relatively small. Ethnic and other groups are
asserting themselves in an effort to affirm and prevent their identity
from being absorbed by great corporate power. Again, where will
it all end? Will it mean a crescendo of sporadic violence, more
ethnic and racial warfare? In what direction will the changing align-
ments of power finally lead?

The dilemma is unprecedented because modern civilization is unprecedented in its advanced industrial form. As a dilemma which has arisen out of unprecedented power and which has put the destiny of humanity in doubt as never before, it is essentially a religious dilemma. This has already been suggested by the various parallels or affinities between dedication to power as a religion and the Judeo-Christian religion, which itself is also a religion of power. The number and character of these are too significant to be dismissed as coincidental. Dedication to power has its own equivalent of monotheism, omnipotence, invisibility or secrecy, omniscience, catholicity (i.e. multi-national), creativity, freedom (equated with power), and eschatology (heaven and hell). A number of questions emerge which deepen the dilemma. To what extent, if any, does dedication to power inherit these characteristics from the Judeo-Christian religion? To what extent are they common to power of any kind? Or, to reverse the question, to what extent if any does the Judeo-Christian religion encourage dedication to power as a religion?

In this respect two observations may be relevant. The first concerns the fact that the early Christian church, which began as a movement among the poor in Palestine, eventually secured surprising prominence and power in the Roman Empire with the conversion of the Emperor Constantine in the fourth century. So the question at once arises: How was it able to do this? What were its strategies? The second observation is best expressed in the words of a distinguished New Testament scholar: "For more than 1 500 years the churches have normally been on the side of the existing ruling order. To that extent they were involved in the wrong, the oppression, the robbery and murder perpetuated by those in power and not infrequently they shared in the profits."[11] It is true, of course, that the churches have had their benevolent projects in aid of the poor and destitute—their inner city missions and their overseas missions—all promoted with a concern for the unfortunate. But these do not diminish the fact that being on the side of the existing ruling order as the normal role of the church for more than 1,500 years has been more of a captivity than freedom—a captivity which has usually been concealed by cooperation with the ruling order. Indeed, it would seem that power attracts power, especially when an eroded Judeo-Christian religion is attracted by sheer dedication to power as another religion of power.

The peculiar fact is that dedication to power of itself has not been generally regarded as a religion. While its parallels or affinities with the Judeo-Christian religion suggest that it is a religion, these have not convinced the public or religious mind. For this reason it has largely remained invisible in its religious character— invisible because of not being classified as a religion. So its classification as a religion has to be further justified.[12] This is necessary if the dilemma is to be better understood and the Invisible Religion of Power exposed as a genuine religion. The first step in this direction is to affirm that the primary motivation of any society, class, or body of people—any individual company, corporation, government, or bureaucracy—that to which they give themselves more or less totally and by which their culture, consciousness, and conduct are definitively conditioned constitutes their real and primary religion. Such religion is called *invisible* for two main reasons. *First,* it is not included under the commonly accepted definition of religion as church-centered with an institutional cultus, commitment to a designated deity (named) and to a formally approved orthodoxy and orthopraxy. *Second,* it is not recognized as a religion even by those who are dedicated to it. They never recognize it as a religion even though their commitment to it is often expressed in ways which have peculiar similarities with formal religion. And even if a passing thought suggests it is religion, they will probably dismiss it as secularism and regard it as religionless, which is really a synonym for its invisibility.

The commonly accepted definition of religion ignores the fact that religion often assumes forms other than church-centered varieties. It ignores the fact that religion often appears as non-institutional mysticism, such as nationalistic folk mysticism, nature mysticism, and even aesthetic mysticism. It also ignores the fact that modern atheism seems more akin to idolatry, and literally as "a-theism" would probably be better described as idolatry when it involves dedication to totalitarianism as a false absolute. Indeed, there is enough of a parallel between devotion to modern dictators and the worship of ancient Pharaohs, Caesars, and kings and their respective despotisms to suggest that idolatry is a better definition than atheism. And idolatry is religion.

Another conclusion further suggests why the dilemma is difficult to define and why such religion is especially capable of captivating the Judeo-Christian religion or any other historical religion of comparable importance. This conclusion is that social change is a form of communication, which in promoting what may be called the missionary outreach of the invisible religion has both positive and negative effects—that is to say, winning some and alienating others. Indeed, social change is largely an invisible form of communication like the invisible religion it propagates. It is invisible in somewhat the same way in which the medium is the message. It conditions the background more than the foreground, the context more than the text, the gestalt more than the constituent part, and the unconscious more than the specific thought. In this way it changes the foreground, the text, the constituent part, and the specific thought with only minimal recognition. They seem the same. They sound the same. But something has changed which is hard to recognize. It is something which modifies the message, specific beliefs, doctrines, and practices of political parties, class and cultural persuasions, educational institutions, and the various forms of church centered religion without anyone really recognizing what is happening. The reason for this is that the message of social change as the invisible communication of power is primarily canopic (enveloping), contextual, and environmental—a field of influence—rather than a specific verbal or printed message. It conditions the whole being, manner of life, and outlook. Its subtle saturative form is more effective than lessons, lectures, sermons, revivals, special appeals, party rallies, conferences, study sessions, or even the daily news.

As thus described, change as a canopic, contextual message of power devaluates language. This is because language is largely a matter of particulars, texts, and specific items which are eroded by such change, again with only minimal recognition. In a word, the continually changing context changes language as the text within the context, so that language serves the interests of power. As a result language is valued less for its content than as an instrument or technique. The obvious examples are propaganda, advertising, public relations, promotionalism, and political campaigns. Talking becomes more a technique in which its truth content is repressed because truth is a threat to power. Instead of the truth which makes the rich and powerful free, it is more often the truth which makes them fear. The emphasis is therefore less upon the *what* than the *how.* Under these circumstances language, including talking, must be done with less emphasis on saying anything than upon the technique of persuasion.

As a further aspect of the way in which language is devaluated, the implosion of programs and news from the media has a saturative, hypnotic effect upon the individual. The amount to see, hear, and read, the quantity of junk mail and bureaucratic reports—the incessant talking—can scarcely have any other effect than to devaluate language. This, along with the explosion of information, tends to swamp the best of minds. The point is eventually reached at which language tends to become a matter of empty words, and dialogue a matter of playing a game. Talking tends to acquire a buzzing effect like a swarm of insects with words cancelling out preceding words and in which all semblance of truth disappears.[13] The whole process becomes highly manipulative, especially if done in a positive, folksy, low key, rhythmic style which is formless and therefore protean, intended only to serve the interests of power.

In the end the devaluation of language signifies the repression of truth. Strangely enough, this happens with the triumph of science, technology, and technique which are emphasized as primarily concerned for truth. But the way they process the truth makes it all the more amenable to power and the resultant devaluation of language. What this means has been clearly expressed in those well known poetic lines "Endless invention, endless experiment . . . where is the wisdom we have lost in knowledge? Where is the knowledge we have lost in information?"[14]

At this point the danger is that the devaluation of language will have an alienating effect upon people at all levels of society and particularly upon those who are insignificant and powerless. It can generate two reactions which can readily combine with each other. The first is a compulsion to find security in a rigid kind of certainty. This can develop into a dogmatic, highly particularized religious and political ideology which is believed with a passionate literalism. The second is a compulsion to find security in subjectivity with a similar emphasis on certainty. This can develop into a dogmatic, highly particularized religious and political pietism, which, in its charismatic dimension, is believed with the same passionate literalism. As evidence of cultural despair these two reactions provide the fertile soil for demagoguery and dictatorship. At the same time they can only accentuate the captivity of the church to power. They, like the power against which they react, are a similar kind of power—a negative form which likewise represses the truth. At this stage, as in the whole proliferation of modern power, the most urgent need is to reveal the truth which has been repressed—a task which requires the courage of a prophet and the willingness to suffer the consequences. And even this may not suffice in the end, given the technology and technique by which a prophet can be silenced.

It is now appropriate to provide a brief orientation to the next four chapters which deal with the major respects in which the church is being infiltrated by such religion and to a surprising extent captivated by it. The emphasis in each instance is upon the *subliminal* and the *integrative* and therefore upon what is generally unrecognized. In chapter two, "The Ecumenism of Power" concerns the monopolistic ("monotheistic") consolidation of power at the center (bureaucratic headquarters) and its regional, national, and multinational expansion outwards ("catholicity," "mission") in what amounts to a merger movement. As this infiltrates government, industry, education, and organized religion, it tends to integrate them both separately and collectively into one enormous complex (unity). Chapter three, "The Conversion of the Individual," concerns his personal commitment to the Invisible Religion of Corporate Power which is sufficiently similar to Christian conversion that the two tend to blend into one. As this happens he is more easily captivated by such religion because he serves it most of his time, but the church only a mere fraction of his time. So he tends to adapt the latter to the former in a subliminal manner. In chapter four, "Justification by Success," the tendency to blend Christian salvation into the kind of salvation provided by the Invisible Religion of Corporate Power is even greater. This is not only because success is so easily seen as the favor ("grace") of God but because success elevates the social status of the individual both in the church and presumably in the sight of God. In these respects Christian salvation is both infiltrated by success and integrated into it as a form of "salvation." In chapter five, "The Invisible Sin" is the kind of sin by which the church is infiltrated and captivated in the subtlest manner of all. As the sin which thereby moves into the life, work, message, and worship of the church in the most subliminal manner of all, it resembles a secret infection of some strange "sickness" which is generally neither recognized nor diagnosed.

2.
the ecumenism of power

The invisible religion of power has its own peculiar form of ecumenism. This varies according to the type of unity which best serves its interests under a given combination of circumstances. It may be an association, a federation, a union, a corporation, a totalitarian state, or some other comparable form. As power increases both in magnitude and variety, the need of integration and coordination increases in the direction of monopolism as the ultimate form of ecumenism. In the modern situation in which unprecedented social change reflects unprecedented power, particularly that of science, technology, and technique, the trend towards this ultimate form of ecumenism has reached unprecedented proportions. It is moving toward a global dimension which means a greater global interdependence and cooperation and therefore a greater trend towards one world and one world religion, albeit the invisible religion. It is thus fulfilling more than ever before the inherent "monotheistic" logic of such religion that all should be one.

For a contemporary study of the ecumenism of power, scarcely a better example can be selected than that of America as the most advanced industrial society in the world. The extent to which it has appropriated science, technology, and technique has distinguished it in many important respects as prototypical of what other industrial societies may yet become. Just as the older, individualistic (entrepreneurial) capitalism manifested itself in the sectarian and denominational form of the invisible religion, so the newer corporational, monopolistic form of capitalism manifests itself in the ecumenical form.[1] It is this latter form which, by its integration of systems into systems in the name of efficiency, has achieved new levels of production and eliminated wasteful competition and "sinful" divisions.

The compulsion towards such ecumenism manifests a double dimension. As each company or corporation expands outwardly and becomes larger and larger, it consolidates itself at the center as a necessary means of coordinating and controlling the whole operation. This means that the expansion is accompanied by a corresponding centralism.

Geographically speaking, the expansion on an urban, suburban, national, and multi-national scale is largely facilitated by technology. It is mainly the result of modern transportation and communication. It would not be possible on such a scale, however, if the only means of transportation were rowboats, horses, buggies, and wagons, and the only means of communication that of couriers using such transportation. Under these conditions there could be only local expansion. There could be no national or multi-national corporations, no national or international federations of labor, and no national or world councils of churches. But the expansion is also the result of the extent and variety of specialization, including the equipment and processing which this involves—again facilitated by technology. This has expanded the need and search for natural resources just as it has expanded the production and sale of products. At the same time the character of such expansion in its advanced industrial form has multiplied the degree and complexity of centralism, as evidenced in specialized departments and administration. Such centralism is symbolized by the head office of the company or corporation at a specific geographical location with its bureaucratic hierarchy and power elite.

The same compulsion with its double dimension has been evident in the various levels of government. They have expanded the scope of their operations outwardly while consolidating their power at the center by means of increasing bureaucratic complexity and integration and increasing personnel and managerial expertise. The result has been an increasing expansion of government outwardly along

is to promote monopolism either within such religion or within advanced industrial society, especially because the latter is already dominated by techno-monopolism. In the light of such a combination of tactics, the ancient Constantinian monopolism of the Christian church can be better understood along with its counterparts in subsequent periods of history.

As for the merger movement of companies and corporations, if the government had not intervened and limited the trend toward monopoly—which it did only to a partial extent—the result would have been a complete monopoly in many sectors of the economy. In this respect the government action reflected a concern to preserve democracy while the trend toward monopoly reflected a drive which could eventually end in some form of totalitarianism. The trend toward monopoly which signifies the growth of totalitarianism within the womb of democracy does not base its franchise upon the democratic principle of one vote for each individual, but upon the amount of money each possesses, especially in the form of stocks and other securities. This means that in principle it is totalitarian, which would soon become evident in a situation in which the democratic tradition had seriously eroded under the impact of such monopoly and other causes. This would mean an American federal government based upon the same monopolistic principle of monetary franchise, which, in the final stage, would be enforced by police and military power. It would mean the ultimate in the ecumenism of power—a unity dictated by its imperatives.[12]

As a result of the merger movement and other forms of the ecumenism of power, the casualties among smaller companies and independent business operations were heavy. Thousands of them were absorbed (bought up) or forced out of business or into bankruptcy and financial ruin. They were the victims of what could be fairly described as an economic form of Cold Warfare. The only merciful aspect of the warfare was the absorption (buying up) of those unable to compete. They were at least spared financial ruin.

In this situation the Invisible Religion of Corporate Power was oblivious to any responsibility for the thousands of those who were forced out of business and into financial ruin. As the religion of the winners (the saved), it saw nothing in itself which contributed to the fate of the losers (the lost). It could only see its achievement as good and positive and therefore synonymous with success and progress, which in turn signified the salvation provided by the invisible religion. The winners could not conceive of themselves as sinners. They could only blame the losers as those who themselves were responsible for their lostness, allegedly because of their ineptitude and inefficiency, if not their laziness and indiscretion, which as a partial truth was widely accepted. This meant that the invisible religion of the winners was always a high religion—one high above the losers—which if anything held the losers in contempt. But the alleged sin of the losers and the height (holiness) of the winners had to be concealed or at least kept at a low key in the interest of power. This enabled the winners to keep their heads high and more easily pass by on the other side and not see the wounded losers lying on the road. In this respect their invisible religion was like that of the high ("holy") religion of the priest and Levite in the ancient parable, in contrast to the compassion of the Good Samaritan, the unsaved, excluded one whose religion would not permit him to pass by on the other side.

The development of large expansive corporations which thus eliminate smaller companies and operators is the shape of things to come in the latter part of the twentieth century. As an example of authorities who support this judgment, Andrew Hacker puts it clearly.

"Since the end of the war," says Hacker, "the corporation has emerged as the characteristic institution of American society. Its rise has rendered irrelevant time honoured theories of politics and economics and its explosive growth has created new breeds of men whose behaviour can no longer be accounted for by the conventional rules of conduct. . . . The small business community stands alongside corporate America and still embraces most of the working and entrepreneurial population. . . . Yet all signs are that the future belongs to the great corporate institution. . . . No one can seriously contend that there will be a re-birth of small business. . . ."[13]

In order to appreciate what such a future signifies, it is important to recognize that the large corporation is not an ordinary company merely expanded in size. The crucial point to emphasize is that beyond a certain magnitude it undergoes a certain metamorphosis which gives it the character of a quasi-political state. At this stage the scope and variety of its operations, the status and experience of its officials, and the problems on the minds of its managers closely parallel those of most modern nations. Indeed, in the late sixties fewer than a dozen nations had a gross national product larger than the amount of money handled by the General Motors Corporation in a single year.[14]

As readily expected of corporations of such magnitude, "their influence on formal government, direct or indirect, conscious or unconscious, is enormous." In fact their "influence is so often peremptory that it may be better described as quasi-decretal." Through their agents they "often tell governments what they," the governments, "must do and cannot do."[15] This is why the insight of Bertrand de Jouvenal, a distinguished authority on the subject from the Sorbonne (University of Paris), is especially relevant. "The corporation," he says, "is fundamentally a political organization and one of the greatest errors of political scientists has been their failure to see this."[16]

In view of what has been said about the invisible religion, the parallel insight should be emphasized that the corporation is fundamentally a religious organization. One of the greatest errors of theologians and other religious leaders has been their failure to see this. This means that it is fundamentally a politico-religious organization which assimilates its economic function to this role. The late David Roberts of Union Theological Seminary, New York City, saw the corporation as a religious organization, indeed, as exemplifying the wider pattern of a creeping totalitarian religion. He emphasized that it dictated how a man dedicated to it finds security, self esteem, standards of value, and reasons for living. He emphasized how it tended to determine the location of a man's home, his home life, the kind of wife he should have, and the overall pattern of his life. While some mobility was permitted within the pattern, such a man "lost the basic freedom of departing from the pattern itself."[17] Roberts could have added that the corporation, as a legalized impersonal entity with rights similar to those of the private individual and which at the same time develops a corporate social image as basic to its operation, is to a large extent a legalized idol. It is not a person, yet it is treated as if it were one—a special one to which vast numbers of people are dedicated to a degree which resembles that given to such ancient idols as Jupiter and Zeus. Its advantage over these ancient idols is its appropriation of science, technology, and technique in achieving miracles of innovation and production and unprecedented profits, and therefore of winning a deeper dedication from its followers than these ancient idols ever could. The question which Christians have never faced, especially in suburbia—a sector of society to which the corporations have largely contributed and where the main line denominations are predominately based—concerns breaking out of what Winters calls *the suburban captivity of the churches.* This is a matter of deciding to what extent dedication to Christ is compatible with dedication to a company or corporation. Is dedication to Christ merely a privatized, subjectivized dedication, and therefore a secret, or is adaptation to the objective power of a company or corporation the primary dedication?

As a further development in the ecumenism of power, Jouvenal's insight is confirmed by the extent to which the American corporations have tended to integrate with the federal government and reveal their essentially political nature. It is sufficiently evident to John Kenneth Galbraith, the Harvard economist, that such integration has been the most significant change in American society since the Second World War.[18] It has largely arisen from new sophisticated science and technology, war research and production, and the stimulation of the economy which have been so essential to America in its new international role since the war. In each of these areas the resources of the federal government have been indispensable. Thus, in contrast to the fear of government interference typical of business a few generations ago, the opposite mood now prevails. The attitude was fostered by the success of government war expenditure in ending the great depression of the thirties.[19] Business now welcomes government assistance in such forms as subsidies, tax exemptions, depletion allowances, and controlled interest rates. It looks to the government for developing vital sectors of the economy and for providing large and lucrative contracts for war supplies and equipment.

Reference to these contracts introduces a further aspect of the integration of corporations with the federal government. Large numbers of corporations have become virtually integrated with the

Defense Department (Pentagon) of the federal government in what has become known as the Military-Industrial Complex. It was President Eisenhower who drew attention to this complex and its potential danger in a warning that has been often quoted. He warned the nation to be on "guard against the acquisition of unwarranted influence, whether sought or unsought, by the military-industrial complex." He further said that "the potential for the disastrous rise of misplaced power persists and will persist" and that it "is felt in every city, every state house, every office of the federal government." What is not as often quoted is that Eisenhower also warned against the danger that "public policy could itself become the captive of a scientific-technological elite."[20] This of course was the elite which was so essential to the development of the arms industry and to what Galbraith calls the technostructure of corporate power.

The nature of this integration represented by the Military-Industrial Complex may be better appreciated from Galbraith's description, which applies here as it does in other areas of the close association of the corporations with the federal government. "No sharp line separates government from the private firm. . . . Each organization is important to the other; members are intermingled in daily work; each organization comes to adapt the others goals; each adapts the goals of the other to its own. Each organization is accordingly an extension of the other."[21] In such an integration, it has been primarily the interests of the corporations which have been served by the other participants, even though much has been ostensibly said and done in the name of national interest. To a surprising extent, the federal government has accommodated itself to the interests of the corporations, including its foreign aid program and its foreign policy.[22] The same can be said of the military and the scientific-technological elite and the universities and institutes of technology which have supplied this elite. Both directly and indirectly, the latter have served the interests of the corporations and profited by lucrative war contracts, especially in research. Indeed, by the mid-sixties from 75 to 100 colleges, universities, and institutes of technology had war contracts with the federal government through the Defense Department.[23] For this reason it would be appropriate to speak of the Military-Industrial Complex as the Military-Industrial-University Complex.

It is peculiar that Galbraith in his *New Industrial State* (1967), where his major thesis deals with the integration of the federal government and the corporations in terms of what he calls the technostructure, failed even to mention the concern which President Eisenhower expressed in his warning about such integration. Nor did he express any concern for the threat posed by a scientific-technological elite. This failure may have been partially explained by a prepossession with the concept of a mature corporation, which seems to deserve a more critical examination than Galbraith provided. What lends support to this explanation of the failure was that two years later he expressed concern on "how to control the military" in a small booklet by this title, but which did not provide an adequate answer. In effect it was more of an indirect acknowledgment of the danger Eisenhower and others have seen, and by implication a question of how mature the developed corporation actually is and what the term "maturity" actually means in this context.[24]

All of this integration designated by the Military-Industrial-University Complex and beyond the Complex in other areas was facilitated by the multi-national expansion of American corporations into the vacuum left behind by the declining colonial empires following the Second World War. This was particularly true of the declining British Empire. Such an enormous economic opportunity was all the more quickly seized because America was the one dominant power in a world which had been seriously disarrayed. It was not only an opportunity for the corporations to acquire and develop business and industrial enterprises and to maximize profits, but to appropriate rich natural resources, including minerals, at a time when America had seriously depleted its own supply due to a century or more of prodigality.[25] For these purposes the protective umbrella provided by the American armed forces throughout the world and military aid to "friendly" foreign governments were indispensable. The umbrella consisted of several thousand army, air, and naval bases around the world, several hundred of which were major bases. Associated with these was the world's largest air force and the world's largest navy and probably the world's largest nuclear striking force. The military aid was provided to at least fifty different countries, a large proportion of which were in the Third World. The effect was generally that of promoting a new form of colonialism which tended to perpetuate or worsen already serious poverty and adverse social conditions.[26]

Under these circumstances the corporations spread out into most of the continental areas of the world on a multi-national dimension. Like the tentacles of a giant octopus, they spread out into Canada, Latin America, Britain and Europe, Africa, the Middle East, South and Southeast Asia, and Australia. Wherever there was military and economic cooperation, their activities were kept at a low key (anonymous) level. Where there was not such cooperation a dictatorial government would be encouraged or imposed by means of military and financial aid.

As a result the multi-national corporations gradually acquired such power that their influence challenged the viability of the nation state as it has never been challenged before.[27] Since most of them were American-based and integrated to a surprising extent with the federal government, their influence challenged the viability even of the United States itself as a nation state. The problem arose out of the self-autonomy of the corporations as loyalty to their own power, including the maximizing of profits, came into conflict with loyalty to the nation and the good of the people as a whole. Their ability to influence political parties and elected representatives in one way or another and their role in the process of government itself had reached a magnitude where it was seriously eroding the democratic tradition in the direction of totalitarianism. They were becoming too powerful for any nation state to exercise adequate control over them, especially in view of their ability to infiltrate the power of the state from within. They shifted various phases of their operations from one nation to another to avoid newly adopted controls or to secure advantages such as cheap labor, tax concessions, and exploitable resources which smaller countries often provided more out of weakness than of strength. They shifted these readily out of the U.S. itself if the profit in manufacturing their products in another nation and importing them back into America was obviously to their advantage. In what has become more recently a trend, they shifted their profits into the money markets of the world and exploited the differences of exchange from one currency to the other, thus contributing to world monetary problems.

In these multi-national operations of the corporations, the invisible religion of power moved considerably closer toward a global dimension of ecumenism. As already indicated, this meant a greater global interdependence and cooperation and therefore a greater integration in the direction of one world and one world religion. To a surprising extent, the multi-national corporations were providing a global network which defined the context within which a large proportion of the nations had to live and work and find a common unity. Since the emphasis almost everywhere in the world was increasingly put upon science, technology, and technique, particularly for economic reasons, the corporations found a common factor of crucial importance in dealing with varying types of political and social systems. The ideology implicit in science technology and technique is common to Capitalism, Socialism, and Communism and appeals to the nations of the Third World.[28] It is a common factor which tends to erode their specific ideological characteristics into its own definitive form and thus to bring them closer together. This does not mean that serious differences have declined but only that a common practical form of ideology gives promise of a common interest and solution. Indeed, it is felt in many quarters that the incredibly dangerous knowledge generated by science, technology, and technique can actually contribute to peace and unity, especially when nations and corporate powers recognize that the final alternative is between one world or no world—between the ecumenism of power or the ecumenism (unity) of nothingness.

As already indicated in chapter one, and which can now be developed in the present context of global multi-national corporate integration, interdependence, and cooperation, there is emerging a countervailing trend. The new trend began with the pressure of particularities to break out of the ecumenism of power and assert their freedom. These include a wide range and variety of national, ethnic, racial, and religious bodies and movements, each concerned with affirming its identity and preventing it from being absorbed into some form of dominating and repressive whole. Each tends to see the ecumenism of power as leading to some form of technological totalitarianism which in the end could become a form of (Orwellian) globalism.[29] Each tends to see the integrative, unifying power of such ecumenism as alienating and exploitative, either in the context of unprecedented affluence or in the context of imposed poverty, including that of the new colonialism of the Third World.

As a result, a surprising number of new nations have emerged along with those whose natural resources have recently given them power to assert themselves in gaining a freedom and recognition they had not previously had. At the same time various kinds of liberation movements, countercultures, and separatist nationalistic, racialistic, and sectarian movements have also emerged. But the most important trend which may be easily overlooked is the yearning of the lonely, isolated individual in the technopolitan mass society for the kind of freedom which will provide positive affirmation of his personal identity and worth.[30] The fun culture, designed to interest and control him, not only does not answer his need but alienates him further.

What the individual wants is really signified by another collection of beliefs and characteristics of the Christian religion. They contrast rather sharply with those which, under certain conditions, contribute to monopolism or at least to something akin to it. These include *freedom,* defined as reverence for the high (particularity of the personal), and therefore deliverance from everything, including evil which stands in the way of it. They include *diversity* as a product of freedom, and therefore a characteristic which stands in contrast to inclusive, repressive wholeness when the latter is a function of power and monopoly. They include *love* distinguished by the biblical Greek term *agape,* which in its unconditional outreach and concern for the individual not only contributes to freedom but to that unique *community* with others signified by another biblical Greek term *koinonia.* Such community is a highly important factor in overcoming the loneliness of the individual who suffers from the isolation and insignificance typical of the modern, technopolitan mass society. And finally there is *the omnipotence of God,* which means the complete opposite of those conceptions of it which are merely expanded projections of the power of nature and man and especially that of his science, technology, and technique. Instead, the omnipotence of God, as Søren Kierkegaard beautifully emphasizes, so takes itself back in the giving of itself that it makes the individual free. At the same time it reveals to him a goodness that is absolute and truly creative and by its nature gentle and loving. In other words it is the unique omnipotence of God.[31]

But as the answer to the yearning of the lonely, isolated individual in modern technological mass society, such freedom, diversity, love, community, and omnipotence seem virtually impossible to find. Will he go to the "neighbor" next door who is a stranger and remains a stranger? Will he seek it from his fellow worker on the assembly line, in the office, or at a meeting or conference when all are preoccupied with prescribed duties and their time preempted? Will he go to the Inner City Mission where he will be fed and exhorted but only find more of his kind? Will he find it in the "friendly," busy church where organization is substituted for community (koinonia) and activities and a changing membership prevent anyone from really coming to know and care for another, where all remain virtually strangers to one another despite the worship and prayerful atmosphere? Will he turn to God when the power god is so overpowering?

All of this concerns not only the future of the individual but the future of society and civilization itself, as lonely, isolated, insignificant masses of people become desperate in their deep yearning for these uniquely, positive, human, and sacred qualities. It involves the future of these individual and community qualities in an increasingly technological world which, though providing its own equivalent of them, is at the same time the greatest threat to them. For many it means that the greatest threat to the individual comes from the mystery of man—the collective man without and the hidden man within—in which man is against himself, in contradiction with himself. This in turn is magnified in the present time both by the technological promotion of progress and the technological generation of alienation as an extreme form of the contradiction. Many are wondering if the latter will eventually mean the fulfilment of Kierkegaard's prophetic warning that "in the end all corruption will come from the natural sciences."[32]

As a result, there is a deep yearning within the individual for deliverance from himself and for the acquisition of true identity, and as a result participation in the most tangible expression of those beliefs and characteristics which have been outlined in such a posi-

tive manner—freedom, diversity, love, community and the true omnipotence of God. In this yearning there is a nostalgia for the
Absolute which can eventually enable the individual to become a
genuine person in a genuine community. In a word, he longs to be
delivered from the power of man and of man's world, and even from
that of himself, all of which the ecumenism of power has made both
so threatening and attractive. At this point the temptation to worship
the false absolute of power as an answer to this nostalgia may be
especially appealing. At the point of deepest yearning for the God
of Love can often come the deepest temptation of yielding to a false
God, especially to the power god with all its subtle and positive
fascination.

3.
the conversion
of the individual

The invisible religion involves the conversion of the individual as a basic condition of faith and obedience. Like other forms of religious conversion, this has two important aspects: a change of direction and a transformation. The change of direction means that the person's life no longer revolves around himself but around the power to which he is dedicated. The transformation means that his life is changed in depth and style to serve the interests of such power. As a result, the spirit of such power enters into him and possesses him so that he is energized to work with a drive which contributes to its success and to his own fascination with what it does. Its ethos and its imperatives captivate his life so that he surrenders himself to it as his new self-identity. In this respect he becomes a new person—different from what he was before—and therefore a converted person.

What the conversion signifies is that the power to which he gives himself in such a manner—be it a corporation, a government, a political party, a military or ecclesiastical body—conditions him to conform to it in a positive manner and find fulfillment in obedience to its requirements. In general this was what social research found in the fifties in the typology of the "other-directed,"[1] "organization" man.[2] It found that the typical American was more the dependent man of the new managerial society of advanced industrialism than the independent man of the old democratic agricultural society who was influenced by the traditional self-initiative typical of the pioneer. This new dependent man was typical, of course, of the large extent to which America had become an urbanized, mass society, which could be more accurately described as technopolitan and therefore a highly organized society. Its dominate corporate nature as contrasted with the older, individualistic rural society symbolized by the family farm was reflected in the categories of employment at the mid-century (1950). By this time 85 percent of the work force were employed by others, 50 percent of whom were employed by large organizations, while only about 15 percent were self-employed. At the same time less than 10 percent of the total population worked on family farms, in contrast to about 50 percent in 1900. Yet the tradition of the independent, democratic individual continued as the popular ethos, more as a myth than a reality, probably because it served the interests of corporate power to keep the tradition alive.[3]

The so-called new "other-directed," "organization" man who was characterized by conformity rather than independence was actually anything but new. In ancient times, for example, the thousands of slaves who built the pyramids in Egypt were characterized by conformity in their devout obedience to the Pharoahs as divine. They were converted to their god and deeply dedicated to him. The same could be said of modern armies dating back to the eighteenth century, at which time they became more correlated with the organizational character of machines. The regimentation, drill, uniforms, obedience, loyalty, and precision were characteristics which made the soldier a typically "other-directed," "organization" man who lived in conformity to what was required of him.[4] His conversion to the army and patriotism was reinforced by the positive as indicated by loyalty and dedication, along with color, music, status, public esteem, and honor. It was essentially a religious conversion with the God to which it appealed more of a patron and legitimizer of its power than anything else. The emphasis was on glory, which, as Eric Hoffer emphasizes, is largely a theatrical concept. The rituals, ceremonies, processions, and parades caused the individual to forsake himself and identify wholly with the act, and in true theatrical fashion to become vividly aware of the vast audience applauding him.[5]

This emphasis on the theatrical leads somewhat naturally into another important factor which in contemporary America has contributed to the conformity of the "other-directed," "organization" man. This is the so-called *graphic revolution* which has produced a visual culture in which images are virtually invitations to conformity. The advent of motion pictures, television and advertising, public relations, and the importance of packaging and marketable personalities, as well as the enormous emphasis on tourism and the popularity of photography, have had this effect. Any notable organization develops an image, especially a corporation which sees the value of a socially positive image as a means of promoting sales. This pertains as much or more to its various products because the customer is so largely conditioned to buy an image including models, designs, and styles. In this context it is not surprising that the hypnotic appeal of an image has taken the place of a persuasive argument in securing the conversion of the individual not only to a product but to a significant power. In this role the image of such power is in principle no different from the role of any ancient Pharaoh and Caesar, or any modern emperor and dictator. It is all done with such an emphasis on the positive and theatrical, culminating in glory as the aura of power, that any individual, particularly one who is isolated and lonely in a mass society, finds it hard to resist. In this respect it has mass appeal.

Moreover, in the contemporary visual culture the implosive character of the mass media predisposes the individual to identify with imagery and therefore to become "other-directed" and conform. Since the communication is almost totally one-directional, it comes in upon him from the outside so that he is relatively passive, as one who is entertained and therefore consumes what he hears and sees.[6] As a result of his intuitive identification with such communication, he is conditioned psychologically in a manner which to a surprising extent is a form of addiction. This is partly because the communication, particularly that of advertising, involves various kinds of persuasive techniques based upon motivational research.[7] By means of these he is psychologically manipulated in terms of the medium to become "other-directed" and conform to the expectations of his persuaders.

In this process he acquires an openness to the wide variety of persuaders who utilize the media. Indeed, the "other-directedness" of the "organization" man typical of the visual culture is synonymous with such openness. The obvious purpose of such openness is the economic one of being open to the mass persuasion which promotes the mass consumption required by mass production. In this respect the "other-directed" man is the new mass consumer who has acquired the kind of openness which serves such a purpose. He is open to the appeal of the advertisers and salesmen, the promoters and developers, the administrators and analysts, the politicians and financiers—indeed to any kind of social manipulator and expert eager to have a hearing. This openness which they all expect serves the kind of freedom which they themselves possess in taking such initiative. But it erodes the freedom of the "other-directed" man whose openness is so often a measure of his loss of freedom. And yet his loss of freedom in this respect, which is a surrender of himself, indeed a surrender of what might be called his old and now unmarketable inner-directed self, has a curious analogy with conversion as related in the annals of traditional religion. There is always a surrender of an old, if not an unwanted self, which is tantamount to the kind of self that is unmarketable and therefore unacceptable. There is always a losing of an old self, a dying to such a self followed by a finding of a new self, which means a living self—one that means satisfaction and fulfillment. (Cf. Matt. 10:39; Luke 17:33.) In any case, whatever the identity of the power or God to which he surrenders his old self— whatever the form of conversion—the orientation is always that of "other-directedness" because the power or God is "other" than himself. The more transcendent the God the greater the emphasis on "otherness."

Such conversion is always more effective when more emphasis is placed upon the personal, inasmuch as the losing of an old self and the finding of a new one is by its very nature a personal experience. This suggests why the personality market has developed in recent times and has become so effective as a context of conversion. Erich Fromm's classic description of this context and the commodity value of personality will indicate what is meant.

> Man does not only sell commodities, he sells himself and feels himself to be a commodity. The manual laborer sells his physical energy; the business man, the physician, the clerical employee, sell

their "personality." They have to have a "personality" if they are to sell their products and services. As with any other commodity it is the market which decides the value of these human qualities, yes even their very existence. . . . Thus, the feeling of self-confidence, the "feeling of self" is merely an indication of what others think of the person. . . . If he is sought after, he is somebody; if he is not popular, he is simply nobody. The dependence of self esteem on the success of the "personality" is the reason why for modern man popularity has this tremendous importance.[8]

The emphasis here upon the individual "being sought after" is particularly important because, as Fromm indicates, it makes the individual feel that he is somebody. It means that he is of value to the power which seeks after him. It gives him self-esteem. It illustrates what happens to the young college student who in his graduation year is interviewed and sought after by the representatives of a corporation. It heightens his awareness of his personal worth. It contributes to his conversion inasmuch as he often gives himself to the corporation for the rest of his life. In such a personal surrender he finds a comfortable berth within the corporation and a degree of security he would never find on the basis of his own limited resources. Again, there is a curious analogy with the concept of conversion in traditional religion, in which the lost or isolated individual is sought after by the Shepherd God who takes the initiative. (Cf. Luke 15:3–6.) The fact the individual is sought after and considered of value in the eyes of such a God gives him self-esteem and a feeling of being somebody. In the special context of traditional religion, its evangelism thus has a peculiar parallel with the personality market. If the Shepherd God did not take the initiative and the individual respond to him with an appropriate "other-directedness" there would be no conversion and no heightened awareness of personality.

Undoubtedly much has been made of the impersonal character of the conformity typical of the "other-directed," "organization" man. Much has been said of his life of obedience, which includes regularity at work, adhering to instructions, following the program, and never questioning the source or destination of any order. This has been seen as an automatism which serves the interest of bureaucratic objectivity. Indeed, the point has often been emphasized that any bureaucratic system cannot operate efficiently if personal factors such as warmth and friendship, favoritism, and emotionalism characteristic of spontaneous primary groups are allowed to have any significant place in its operation. As a rationally organized social system, any bureaucracy is said to distinguish sharply between the duties inherent in any office and the temptation to enter into personal relationships of any kind which, because they are personal, tend to erode its capacity to operate effectively. How then can it be said that an individual is converted in a personal manner to any organization of this description, especially to a corporation which because of its size and complexity is inevitably bureaucratic?

The explanation for this apparent anomaly may be found in several considerations of the character of large, bureaucratic organizations which have been often overlooked. The first goes back to the character of any modern army which, in spite of its regimented, machine-like operation and style, puts a strong emphasis upon the positive—which in turn has a strong personal appeal. This at once calls to mind that most large organizations, especially companies and corporations, have their own equivalent of such an emphasis upon the positive. They have their corporate image, their rituals of loyalty and personal respect, their atmosphere of courtesy and friendship, and their recognition of faithful service. This means that personal dedication is no more incompatible with an apparent machine-like routine than it characterizes an army. The important consideration in any large organization, as it is in any army, is the morale of its personnel. Unless this be positive and motivating and therefore personal, no organization, however bureaucratic, can operate with efficiency for very long.

This important fact has been increasingly recognized as companies and corporations have become larger and more complicated and their personnel more transient and uprooted in a rapidly expanding urbanized, mass society. There has been a new and comparable emphasis on the human side of management.[9] The result has been that marked attention has been given to those personal categories of appeal which contribute to morale and achievement among the predominant class of employees today. These can be generally described as "knowledge workers" in contrast to the "blue collar" industrial worker of a generation ago, or the farmer of a generation or two earlier. This means that attention is given to such personal categories of appeal as status, career, community, specialization, security, and various kinds of fringe benefits. The collective impact is of such a nature that it enables the "knowledge worker" to identify in a more deeply personal manner with his company or corporation and find fulfillment in its operation.

As evidence of this human side of management, in which there has been a shift from the older, somewhat impersonal emphasis on contract to the more personal emphasis on status, along with an emphasis on community and various fringe benefits, Andrew Hacker gives a variety of fascinating examples.

"By now," he says, "we know all about the social facilities provided by the large corporations. Eastman Kodak's medical plans, IBM's country clubs, Richfield Oil's model homes, du Pont's psychiatrists, Reynolds Tobacco's chaplains, and even RCA's neckties and their corporate insignia—all are symptomatic of the concerted effort to create a feeling of community within the corporation."[10]

All of this means that the conversion of the individual in a deeper dimension of personal dedication is much better sustained by the equivalent of what, in biblical terminology, is meant by the community of faith. In this respect the corporation covenants with its personnel to provide the kind of positive fellowship which will sustain their faith in it and in one another and which will contribute to the enrichment of their conversion experience. It will be anything but automaton conformity.

What this deeper dimension of personal dedication can mean in the context of such fellowship (and which makes the corporation seem more like a church than a bureaucratic organization, and in fact reinforces the idea that it is essentially a religious organization) is vividly described by Harrington under the title of "Life in the Crystal Palace."[11] He describes his experience as a member of the staff of a corporation head office located in the lush surroundings of a comfortable suburb. They were like a happy family living in an atmosphere of comfort and courtesy. Life was good and gentle with each doing his work in a leisurely manner amid smiling faces and amiable superiors. The emphasis was upon team play and the importance of getting together and talking things over, with each one contributing his mite. Conformity was more by personal choice in the midst of deepening contentment than by anything else. It was not forced or imposed. Everyone was provided with a pension fund, an inexpensive medical program, a low premium life insurance policy, assistance in moving and buying new homes and in the daily expense of lunches. At noon there were movies in the auditorium, an opportunity to visit the library and to watch color television or play darts or table tennis in the game room. There was a corporation store and a lunchroom staffed by friendly waitresses. Harrington comments that, if anything, the friendly familial, comfortable life was far from being a threat to the ego of any employee. It instead tended to atrophy the ego through disuse. A little more tension would have been welcome. It would have given more reality to the sublimity of what was literally life in a "Crystal Palace." And yet what Harrington should have recognized was that the fascination with such a life was the secret, positive appeal by which the corporation not only converted the individual employee but secured his dedicated surrender to it as the object of his devotion.

This should also be recognized as the explanation—at least in part—of that strange willingness of the individual to surrender his freedom which attracted the interest of Dostoevsky. The explanation of this surrender, which is involved in the conversion of the individual to any corporate power, is not wholly provided by the various factors which to this point have been cited as undoubtedly contributing to it. In this fascination with the positive aspect of corporate power is imbedded the deeper fascination of the individual for any kind of power which promises him a new and wider identity by his surrender to it. Dostoevsky emphasized the burden of "conscience" or the burden of responsibility, and therefore the gamble involved in the exercise of individual freedom which is necessarily costly if the individual has few resources or friends upon which to depend. Under these conditions, which are well nigh universal, the individual is fearful of his freedom and all the more fascinated with any other individual with power. Beyond this, he is fascinated with any corporate power to which he can surrender himself and therefore his freedom. As a factor contributing to any form of conversion this is one which is always very important.

In his penetrating insight into this mystery of individual freedom,

Dostoevsky put it in these familiar words: "Man is tormented by no greater fear than to find someone quickly to whom he can hand over that gift of freedom with which he is born. . . ."[12] Ordinarily, of course, freedom is conceived as that for which man strives if necessary to the point of struggling long and hard and exercising incessant vigilance to preserve. It is ordinarily seen as having a great positive appeal for which man longs as the fulfillment of himself and his deep, inward creativity. As something existential, it is seen as the fulfillment of an anterior sinecure of essence. But Dostoevsky does not see it in this positive light. Instead, he sees it as a burden and therefore as negative, which is often more realistic in view of the readiness with which man is converted to corporate power. If, however, there is any weakness in Dostoevsky's profound insight, it is that he did not emphasize the positive fascination with power which man so generally confuses with freedom. Thus, in the context of the unprecedented power typical of contemporary society, it could almost be said that modernity signifies the equation of freedom with power, and that the most widespread form of religious conversion is that of the individual surrendering to such fascination. This pertains both to sudden and to gradual conversion, as the individual yields to such fascination in order to find a greater identity which is not his own but which he thinks is his own.

It is now appropriate to focus attention upon the *unconverted,* which again is a further development of the other side of the distinction made in chapter one between the winners and losers, the overclass and the underclass. Generally speaking, the unconverted include the losers, the unsuccessful, the disillusioned, the powerless, the insignificant, the poor, and the unskilled. In such a general description of those who are not converted to the invisible religion (and in this respect are still unsaved), there is one fact to emphasize at the outset. The unconverted not only approximate the lower classes but are found in surprising numbers in all other levels of society. The reason for this multi-level lack of faith in the invisible religion is the increasing anti-modernity which has arisen in recent times for a variety of reasons. Among these are such serious matters as dangerous knowledge, all the reasons given in chapter one, among which are depletion of resources, pollution of the environment, population explosion, urban crisis and sprawl, and the finitude

of the life support potential of the earth. These problems are disillu-
sioning people at every level of society and making them skeptical
of the invisible religion, especially in its espousal of technology in
combination with big money and military power. They see the invisible religion as mainly responsible for this crisis of modernity and yet
do not know where to turn for a practical solution.

As a result of such multi-level skepticism, the unconverted not
only include the old middle class with its small farmers, local mer-
chants and independent professionals, but even more typically the
dropouts from every level of society. The latter contribute to what
may be described as the discard heap at the bottom of the social
scale, which to a surprising extent the old middle class for all their
skepticism tend to hold in contempt. The old middle class, for all that
may be said of its declining power and sense of loss, is still influenced by the work ethic and a certain disdain for dropouts.

Nevertheless, the discard heap at the bottom of the social scale
is a significant reflection of what is happening in advanced industrial
society and probably a highly important omen for the future. Gunnar
Myrdal sees this segment of society as the typical product of high
technology. Since such technology requires more specialized education for employment, it increasingly dispenses with the services of
those who are unskilled or handicapped by locality, race, opportunity, and poverty. Myrdal speaks of such a class of unemployed or
unemployable as a structural substratum in American society which
is generally ignored by the great sources of power. He emphasizes
that the fact that such a substratum is "not very articulate" and
therefore "little noticed" by the well educated and relatively affluent "does not detract from the gravity of this development." He
goes on to say that it is fatal to democracy as such, and not merely
demoralizing for individual members of this class, that they remain
so mute and so devoid of initiative and that they show no sign of
organizing themselves to fight for their interests.[13,14]

The dropouts from all levels of society which add to the discard
heap include derelicts and drifters, drug addicts and alcoholics,
maladjusted and disillusioned, the old and exhausted, and the alienated youth from suburbia. They are the human equivalent of the junk
heap of any technological society—old worn-out rusty cars and
refrigerators, old stoves and washers, old out-moded factory equip-

ment and locomotives. Their attitude, along with those who are the typical product of high technology, is generally one of apathy. This can be understood from their feeling of insignificance and power-lessness. It means that most, if not all, of them have lost interest in trying and are dependent for their subsistence upon welfare agen-cies. At the same time such apathy tends to generate violence, especially among the younger, more vigorous elements whose alien-ation explodes in what amounts to an unconscious form of protest.

This apathy of the unconverted discard heap is surprisingly con-gruent with the political apathy of the New Middle Class. The latter, which consists largely of status employees who identify with their company or corporation, tend to keep strictly out of politics. They are afraid of offending customers, stockholders, directors, and su-periors. They often do not even think politically, preferring to leave political matters to top personnel who deal directly with political parties and governments anonymously. What this apolitical attitude by such a large segment of the population could ultimately mean for democracy in the event of a national emergency is suggested by a question put by Andrew Hacker: "If a crisis arises, even a relatively mild one, can we be sure that this group will continue to adhere to democratic values?" Then he adds: "The corporation has certainly not set out to weaken the foundations of democratic politics, but its growth as the characteristic institution of our time is having this consequence."[15]

The reason for emphasizing this political apathy of the New Middle Class in association with the apathy of the discard heap is the way in which they mutually reinforce one another. Keeping in mind Myrdal's emphasis on the apathy of the unemployed and unemployable in a technological society as being possibly fatal for democracy, it does not require much insight to recognize that the New Middle Class along with these constitute a majority with the rest of the discard heap. A further cause for concern is that the apathy of these major sectors of society complement the anonymity of the great sources of corporate power. There is scarcely anything that better serves the interests of such power than the prevalence of such public apathy. As a consequence of such apathy, there would be little or no curiosity or questioning and certainly no chal-lenge or determined effort to probe behind the various facades of anonymity to locate and identify the sources of power.

The complementary relationship between the anonymity of these sources and the apathy of such a large proportion of the population parallels the situation which, according to Hanna Arendt, contributed to the rise of National Socialism in Germany. According to her, the German bourgeoisie elite could not have indulged in such "completely unprincipled power politics" (i.e., amoral) "until a mass of people was available who were free of all principles and so numerically large that they surpassed the ability of the state and society to take care of them."[16] The anonymity of the bourgeoisie, whose power operated as secretly as it was unprincipled (amoral), found in the apathy of the masses an unprincipled void or emptiness into which it could move and operate as it pleased. The apathy, which at the same time signified the amorphous character of the masses, meant that they could be effectively manipulated by the bourgeoisie.

Translated into the language of the invisible religion, this meant that they could be "evangelized" more easily than their unconverted condition of life suggested. With a mass appeal in combination with a theatrical demonstration of military power, including color, ceremony, music and action, they could be easily induced to identify with a popular image. As those who secretly cherished within themselves a longing to surrender their freedom—as little as they had remaining in them—they were all the more susceptible to the fascination with power which would fulfill their hope. As a result, they were captivated by the charismatic image of Adolf Hitler, who as a new messiah was amazingly successful in converting them. As the unconverted they were quickly "evangelized" by him and transformed into fanatical devotees of the invisible religion. At this stage the invisible religion broke through the historical and social consciousness and became dangerously visible. It revealed itself for what it was.[17,18]

4.
justification by success

The converted individual as described in the previous chapter feels justified by his success. His satisfaction with his position, status, and benefits convinces him that he has made good and merited his justification (salvation). His new dedication to corporate power and his positive experience of conformity assure him that his conversion has been valid. He is justified by what may be called the philosophy of success. Such philosophy is the equivalent of the law or the will of corporate power which he must obey in order to merit the acceptance of such power. Although this is the equivalent of justification by works according to Christian evangelical theology and therefore self-justification (salvation), the initial and continued action of corporate power in accepting him is a form of grace. This is because the corporate "power god" is not bound by such law to accept him, because such law is largely if not entirely of its own making. The same can be said of its recognition and promotion of him in its hierarchical structure. It is not obliged to do this as if there were a law higher than itself, which in this respect required its obedience. Therefore, its action is equivalent to a form of grace and to this extent the justification (salvation) of the converted individual is by grace.

Although Christian evangelical theology has its roots in the Reformation, and especially in the Pauline Epistles to the Romans

and the Galatians in support of its teaching that justification (salvation) is by grace alone *(sola gratia)*, this has not prevented a certain
popular appeal to selected biblical texts which seem to favor justification by success. A few of these may be cited as examples of how
selected texts can be adapted to this purpose. One of the most
familiar is taken from the Authorized Version with its use of the term
"business" given a market connotation. "Seest thou a man diligent
in his business? He shall stand before kings." (Proverbs 22:29, KJV)
Another example is the reference in Ecclesiastes to God giving
wealth and possessions and power to enjoy them and to accept
one's lot and find enjoyment in one's task—all of which is emphasized as the gift of God (Ecclesiastes 5:19). One final example is
even more emphatic. It concerns the parable of the talents in Matthew 25:14–29, and the parable of the pounds in Luke 19:11–26.
The contrast is between those who invested their money and made
a profit and the one who failed to do this. The former are com-
mended for their success, the latter reprimanded for his failure. He
is considered a wicked servant who in the words of the text is
severely censured: "You ought to have invested my money with the
bankers, and at my coming I should have received what was my own
with interest" (Matthew 25:27; similarly Luke 19:23). In both parables the conclusion is the same: "For to every one who has will more
be given, and he will have abundance; but from him who has not,
even what he has will be taken away" (cf. Luke 19:26). On this basis
the idea of money is seen as something approved by the text and
therefore as a form of meritorious obedience. At the same time it
is seen as the kind of success which is evidence of divine favor and
therefore of grace.

There is little doubt that such texts represent a rather widely held
popular opinion both within and beyond the Christian faith and the
church, the extent of which is difficult if not impossible to assess.
While it is not formally or officially recognized or proclaimed, it
operates somewhat subliminally as a product of the business world
and as a form of the invisible religion. Along with the success of
science, technology, and technique, it accounts for the impression
that the successful segments of society only need God's help to a
limited extent, because they have already justified themselves in his
sight in a substantial measure. They only need his patronage and

legitimation except in crisis situations when they expect all the help
he can give. On the contrary, the impression seems rather widespread that only the unsuccessful such as the poor and the down-
and-outs need salvation wholly by grace alone. They have no
success to their credit in the heavenly ledger and therefore must
depend entirely upon God's favor—in theological terminology—
upon justification by grace alone. The question which therefore
emerges is the extent to which this distinction is reflected in the
correlation of the denominations with the class structure. Are missions and evangelism considered more for the poor and the working
class and less for the rich and the leisure class because the latter
have been already saved to such a large extent by their success?[1,2,3]

It is important, therefore, to examine justification by success as
the kind of salvation typical of the invisible religion of power. This
will be done under three aspects which have been suggested by the
Gospel of John, chapter 14, verse 6, in which Jesus says, "I am the
way, and the truth, and the life." In the invisible religion, success
is substituted for Jesus and therefore itself becomes the Way, the
Truth, and the Life. In developing these three aspects of justification
by success the following themes will be considered:

The Way will be interpreted as the Consumer Style, with an
implicit Cult of the Present.

The Truth will be interpreted as the Objective Style with an
implicit Cult of the Quantum (quantification).

The Life will be interpreted as the Positive Style with an implicit
Cult of the Aesthetic.

The Way as the Consumer Style

As such, it is the way of life in which the individual is dedicated
to the consumption of commodities as an end in itself. The justifying
pleasure and status which this gives to him is obviously in the interests of corporate power which is anxious to maximize its profits and
production. This style means that the individual lives more for the
purpose of consuming than for the purpose of living. It means that
he lives more to eat, drink, clothe himself, and acquire status symbols
than the reverse alternative: to eat, drink, clothe himself, and acquire basic necessities in order to live. As one who is converted and

therefore turned around and changed, his motivation is likewise turned around and changed. This is mainly a result of mass production combined with mass persuasion reaching the stage where it is able to reverse the traditional logic of the market. Instead of the demand for commodities creating a supply, corporate power is of such magnitude that it is able to produce a supply and then create a demand. In a word, it is able to create the Consumer Style of life.

This reversal of the traditional logic of the market by which the individual is conditioned to consume and to feel justified by such success is the result of a combination of factors, most of which are technological. Merely listing them is enough to suggest their collective impact. The first is the mass media which make possible mass persuasion. Then there is the concentration of the masses in the urban areas in close proximity to the supermarkets and shopping plazas. There is also the technique of merchandizing, including packaging and shelving, and a glamorous variety of commodities often accompanied by music which promote impulse buying. And finally there is the unprecedented affluence which provides the facilitating context in which these factors operate. This affluence has virtually reached apocalyptic proportions in its magnitude, with the American Gross National Product rising from approximately 100 billion in 1940 to 1,000 billion (1 trillion) in 1970—a tenfold increase in 30 years, unparalleled in any other nation in the history of the world. Such an increase, which was largely correlated with a war economy, contributed to the rapid increase of the suburban areas which, of all the sectors of society, were most characterized by the Consumer Style. With this in mind, the fact that traditional religion—Protestant, Catholic, and Jewish—so generally migrated to the suburban areas suggests at once how deeply the whole idea of justification by success has infiltrated and conditioned such religion.

The most obvious assumption of the Consumer Style is the equation of freedom with the wide range of options that money can buy. In this conception of freedom, affluence liberates the individual from the old renunciatory style of life which emphasizes hard work, thrift, discipline, sobriety, and chastity. It liberates him from the old ascetic work ethic typical of an economy of scarcity, in which only the most essential goods and services are purchased. It also liberates him from the sacrificial way of life symbolized by the cross in biblical and traditional Christianity. At the same time it liberates him from the belief, doctrine, and creed by which the ascetic, sacrificial life is interpreted and considerably reinforced. Since such belief, doctrine, and creed are too restrictive of the freedom and pleasure equated with purchasing power, they are ignored rather than denied and thus allowed to erode in their particularity. The process of erosion is concealed under the emphasis on feeling, desire, and status typical of the Consumer Style, which in turn blends into the experiential aspect of traditional religion. In other words, traditional religion is transformed into a commodity which can be promoted in such a way that it pleases the people and in effect is consumed by them. Consequently, the new pleasure-orientated "psychological man" typical of the Consumer Style who sits in the pew is there to be comforted, not to be challenged, to be confirmed in his success, not to be convicted of sin. As one who believes in principle that he is liberated from work to leisure and from punishment to pleasure, he wishes to experience the same in the worship, message, and life of the church. He wants to enjoy his religion in a manner comparable to that of buying and consuming commodities. He wants to see his church justified by success and therefore possessed of the appropriate status symbols. He wants it to provide the satisfaction to its members of a wide range and variety of consumer experiences— things which will activate and interest everyone from the youngest to the eldest and thus become a veritable religious shopping center. As a result, therefore, of this whole transformation, the cross is reduced to a liturgical and architectural symbol with an aesthetic appeal which easily blends into the Consumer Style.

The new freedom to buy and consume more, by which the devotee of the Consumer Style feels so justified, is a new freedom to live more fully in the present. It is a freedom to provide as far as possible for immediate gratification. In this respect its invisible religious character qualifies it as a Cult of the Present. It does not measure maturity by delayed gratification but by instant acquisition, instant experience, instant achievement, and therefore of always being up-to-date and abreast with the times. In the context of traditional religion this includes instant communication on the contemporary scene without going back or adhering to the past. It includes instant discussion without prior preparation (discipline), instant fellowship without prior friendship, and therefore instant feeling in one way or another with respect to others.

The assumption, of course, is that an ample supply of goods and services is always there for the asking—easily and quickly available as symbolized by instant foods and beverages. The same is true of sex and entertainment, daily news and information, God and all his blessings. They are considered to be always there for the asking and in quick and attractive packages.

With such an emphasis on immediate gratification, the Cult of the Present is promoted by easy credit on extended terms based upon the principle of buying now and paying later. For this purpose credit cards, charge accounts, "discount prices," trading stamps, contests, prizes, and other means of increasing sales are important. The wider choice of goods and gadgets in varying styles, models, brands, colors, and sizes contribute to the same objective. It all creates the impression that a new freedom has come which is coextensive with such choice and greater than ever before. The experience of euphoria which accompanies the satisfaction of implanted "needs" and "desires" reinforces this impression and tends to become its main component. By means of such a conditioning of behavior and consciousness, the individual is convinced of the validity of the life he is living and believes he is thoroughly justified.

To appreciate better the Cult of the Present, it is helpful to examine two popular and closely related forms of freedom which characterize it. These are:

1. Freedom as an indiscriminate willingness to change.
2. Freedom as an indulgent permissiveness.

The first of these arises largely out of the equation of freedom with purchasing power in which the focus is almost wholly upon the present. As a form of freedom it promotes the interests of the business world, which sees such freedom in terms of a cause-effect relationship. Business determines the prices, the consumer responds; business advertises, the consumer buys. It is a psychological pattern of stimulus-response. Provide the right stimulus and the expected response follows. If in this way people can be persuaded to change their cars every two years and their style of clothing every year and regard such change as freedom, so much the better for mass production. The manufacturers, retailers, and advertisers will readily exploit such freedom. The opinion makers and promoters of peer group specialties will readily cooperate. Everyone and everything will be kept on the move. Cash and credit will be kept turning over like the wheels of industry. For this reason the sales resistance of the consumer must be kept at a minimum. He must be continually softened up, always willing to change and to regard such change as the success and freedom by which he is justified. He must be up to date, in style, possessed of the latest and best, to buy more and consume more and thus provide evidence of his status. He must live fully in the present as if it were the fullness of time which for this reason defines the meaning and purposes of his life. If in the light of such a present as the fullness of time *(kairos)* the consumer be behind, out of style, stuck with the old and obsolete, unable to spend and consume, he must be made to feel guilty and out of it and therefore a sinner. By the implanation of such guilt, he must be made to feel that he is living an inferior, unjustified life and therefore unacceptable to fellow consumers. The problem which this poses for traditional religion—Protestant, Catholic, and Jewish—especially in suburbia is the extent to which such religion is infiltrated by this Cult of the Present and its definition of justification and guilt.

The second freedom is indulgent permissiveness which also serves the interests of the business world in promoting sales in the cultic present. As such it is really only a special form of the first freedom, namely, an indiscriminate willingness to change. Those who change easily in response to salesmen, advertisers, and opinion makers also change in response to their children, students, and parishioners when it comes to moral standards, customs, and other norms. They want their home, school, and church to be up-to-date, in style, abreast with the times, possessed of the best, and to change readily in a permissive manner. If they are parents, they will want their children to have what their neighbor's children have and what their children are only too ready to emphasize that they have. When hardly a day passes without television shows suggesting to children that they badger, wheedle, and pester their parents into buying them something, parents find it difficult not to b permissive. At the same time the erosion of norms and standards, along with the increasing complexity of technopolitan society, makes it difficult for parents to give their children clear and convincing reasons for acting one way and not another. As a way out of their difficulty, parents tend to rationalize their permissiveness by considering it progressive and democratic, often forgetting that a peer group or street gang has already influenced their children in ways that are usually anything but progressive and democratic. As a result the traditional, the historical, and the eternal, as well as the connotation of permanence, are victims of a business-promoted permissiveness just as they are victims of a business-promoted willingness to change —all in the name of freedom and a dedication to consuming as an end in itself. In other words, the individual is made to eat, drink, dress, and consume as the chief end of his life, and to enjoy and praise such fulfillment as the justification of his existence—indeed, as the revelation of the highest good.[4,5,6]

The Truth as the Objective Style

The next aspect or category of success as a means of self-justification is the truth evident in the amazing achievements of science, technology, and technique. Such truth as a remarkable form of success and source of power involves an obvious dedication to objectivity. Ideally, such objectivity is best represented by a scientist working in his laboratory. But it is more widely represented by the individual operating machines in a whole social system of machines, and by his living and working in a society which consists of thousands of organizations more or less integrated into one bureaucratic complex. This, of course, means the development of giant conglomerate cities which are distinctively technopolitan in character. In this context objectivity becomes a style of life and not just the methodology of an individual scientist working in his laboratory. It becomes the style to which the individual is converted as an "other-directed," "organization" man with the openness of one who is also dedicated to the Consumer Style. As one who is dedicated to the Objective Style he finds satisfaction in living in such a society. He feels important because he finds his soul in "knowledge power," in the "know-how" by which he is recognized, accepted, and rewarded, often as a specialist. He accepts the Objective Style as the truth by which he lives. It defines for him "a state of being," that which fills the air he breathes and grips him subliminally in all he says, feels, and does. In this respect the invisible religion has laid hold upon and possessed him.[7]

In saying this it should be emphasized that the Objective Style to which he is dedicated puts more emphasis on power than it does on truth. All objective scientific knowledge, of course, signifies both truth and power. But the more the emphasis is shifted from pure science to technology and technique, the more it is shifted from truth to power. As a result, pure science tends to be repressed by technology and technique and by their correlated bureaucratic managerial establishments. At the same time, objectivity becomes more a means of domination than of liberation. And yet it is this dedication to power in the name of truth and this domination which makes the individual feel so justified. It defines what he means by success.

As a result of the shift of emphasis from truth to power, success tends to be measured more by practical innovation that by independent discovery. This innovation which contributes to business and industry, including the war industry, keeps them highly competitive in the world markets.[8] It is largely promoted by a bureaucracy of scientists and engineers financed by big money. As such the innovation virtually defies description in the production of new technology —machines, equipment, gadgets, synthetic materials, along with the greatest variety of techniques. The latter extend all the way from simple directions to the complex management of systems, organizations, and personnel. A new emphasis on the behavioral sciences contributes to this variety, especially in the management of personnel and beyond this in mass persuasion, including such areas as advertising, public relations, journalism, and politics. A similar observation can be made of church-promoted religion in the wide range and variety of its agencies and operations, its organizations and developments regarding education, congregational life, missions, and evangelism. There is an increasing emphasis on innovation in techniques. It should be emphasized that techniques are truth, just as facts and data are truth, and that they along with technology have given the Objective Style the magnitude of power which has made it such a success. Thus, as a form of truth they are welcomed by church-promoted religion as a contribution to its success as well.

Due to the popular nature of such innovation and the confidence which technology and technique engender in the public mind, a further form of freedom tends to emerge.

The Freedom to Live an Experimental Life

As such it is an extension of the Objective Style of life into areas hitherto considered immune to its influence. It means that the experimental attitude has emerged from the laboratory and entered the marketplace, the neighborhood, the theater, and recreation center, the church and the home, the bedroom and private life of the individual.

There is experimentation on every hand, everyone with everyone else, everyone with something, and generally without the control which the laboratory provides. There is experimentation with sex, nudity, morality, law and order, education, and culture. Everyone is trying out everyone else to see how far they can go— bargaining, manipulating, exploiting, and testing their limits. No area of life is immune from the increasing experimentation which is transforming the whole of society into one vast complicated "laboratory." Again, even in church-promoted religion, in spite of its tradition and loyalty to the past, the same trend towards experimentation is evident in a number of areas. There is experimentation in worship, ministry, communication, education, fellowship, mission, and evangelism. In these various areas the Objective Style is obviously of service to the Consumer Style in satisfying the voracious appetite for something new in the present for immediate gratification. In this respect such church-promoted religion bears some resemblance to those ancient Athenians who spent their time in nothing else but hearing and telling some new thing (cf. Acts of the Apostles 17:21).

At this stage it can be understood how the Objective Style tends to produce what may be called the Cult of the Quantum. As the name suggests, it indicates the stage at which the Objective Style reflects the essential character of the invisible religion, with power becoming an end in itself with a certain mystification. Such a cult is dedicated only to what can be quantified and therefore only to two correlated aspects, namely, the instrumental and that which can be acted upon. On this basis the Truth is of a two-fold nature. On the one hand it consists of the instrumental in its various forms—skills, procedures, methods, and measurements of various kinds which can be generally classified as techniques. On the other hand it consists of a neutral datum—"something" which can be experimented or acted upon, managed and directed, staged and produced, which of course will include facts, data, reports, and studies as well as personnel resources and products. What both sides of this two-fold Truth have in common is "something" which the individual, group, or corporate power have in hand like an instrument or under control like a neutral datum. The common aspect is that of possessing, grasping, controlling, and dominating as evidence of power and success, and therefore is a form of religious fulfillment.

As this Cult infiltrates church-promoted religion, it means a greater emphasis on managed, administered, and designed religion. Services of worship tend to be staged events with a certain resemblance to theatrical productions. The choir, the ministers, and other participants are expected to put on a good performance. Religion is, as it were, a quantum in their possession upon which they act with their various techniques in guaranteeing a good production. God therefore tends to be somewhat of a puppet who is similarly managed and into whose mouth the Cult of the Quantum puts its message. A similar assumption is implicit in the current phrase "the practice of ministry," parallel to the practice of medicine or the practice of law and presupposing a quantum possessed and applied with proper technique. The emerging issue is that of technique as a new and subtle form of legalism which makes the old moralistic legalism seem superficial and elementary. It means that technique is added to grace to achieve justification, to evangelism to secure decisions of faith, in what can ultimately lead to a form of "brainwashing" in the context of what seems serious and holy.[9]

The Life as the Positive Style

The last of the three aspects or categories of success accepted as a means of self-justification is that of the Life understood as the Positive Style. Just as the Way and the Truth lead to Life, so the Consumer Style and the Objective Style lead to the Positive Style. The Life corresponds to the Positive Style because, even in an elementary sense, life is positive in its connotation while the positive generally signifies life. So the two are closely associated. More-

over, the Consumer and Objective Styles have the Positive in common. The one presupposes purchasing power and immediate gratification, which are positive. The other presupposes "knowledge
power" and its fulfillment in action, both of which are also positive.
In other words, the positive factor common to both these styles
involves pleasure. Or, more specifically, the power common to both
styles is productive of pleasure. But beyond the factor common to
both is the recognition that the Positive Style emerges in its own right
as a distinctive style. It transcends the Consumer Style and the
Objective Style to a new level of the Positive with a corresponding
new level of pleasure. This can best be suggested by such terms as
status, class, and rank. It concerns the level of prestige of the
individual in society and in the community and his consciousness of
such prestige. It concerns his new identity which has come by means
of his conversion to the invisible religion in its corporate form. It
involves all the symbols of his new identity and the Positive Style
which reflects and defines it.

At this stage the Positive Style reflects its invisible religious
character as the Cult of the Aesthetic. The important consideration
here is that the aesthetic has a peculiar affinity with power. The two
have a profound association in the strange way in which the aesthetic has a power and fascination of its own, while power has its
own aesthetic value and fascination. To have power and to make
it effective means to a surprising extent that the possessor must
recognize the beauty of power and the power of beauty. This
applies no matter how authoritarian and militaristic the power may
be. It explains why the Cult of the Aesthetic in one form or another
invariably emerges out of corporate power. At this point justification
by success assumes another form—justification by the success of the
aesthetic. This is salvation by means of the beautiful, which is not
entirely unrelated to the beauty of holiness.

Historically speaking, the great corporate forms of power from
the ancient past to the latest modern era have understood this
association of power with the Positive Style and its Cult of the
Aesthetic. They have understood intuitively that an emphasis on the
beauty of power is one of the most effective means of social
control. This has happened because people in all periods of history
and at every social level are attracted to the beautiful in its many

and varied forms and readily identify with it. In this respect the beautiful has probably a wider appeal as a common language than the good and the true. It is therefore no accident in history that the powerful have built their palaces and erected their thrones as well as their cathedrals and their temples. It is no accident that ruling aristocracies, whether political or religious, have developed ritual, liturgy, ceremony, protocol, pomp, show, and manners, accompanied by color, robes and uniforms, and a retinue of servants ready to serve in what amounts to a theatrical version of aesthetic obedience. All of this is one of the most effective means of winning the allegiance of vast numbers of people apart from the positive, prestigious feeling it gives the ruling aristocracy. Thus throughout the ages Pharaohs, Caesars, emperors, kings, popes, bishops, priests, admirals, field marshals, and generals have adopted a positive aesthetic style along with the appropriate color, ritual, and ceremony. In doing this they have generally recognized that music is one of the most important aesthetic ingredients for such a purpose, as evident in the emphasis on bands, organs, and choirs, national anthems, hymns, and folk songs. The total result has been the instillation of respect, awe, and reverence into their subjects as a most effective means of social control.[10]

At times the emphasis on the positive-aesthetic has reached the point of worship as seen in the worship of deified Pharaohs, Caesars, Seleucids, and other rulers. At other times it has stopped short of worship but has approached it in the degree of respect, awe, and reverence expected. This has been suggested by the choice of titles which in effect have elevated the figure in the direction of deification: Majesty, Royal Highness, Excellency, Right Honorable, Holiness, Grace, Venerable, Very Reverend, and Reverend. In this respect, if there is one word to summarize the positive-aesthetic, especially as an essential correlate of power, it is *glory*. Glory has a profound association with power and is basic to its promotion and preservation and if anything is the more important of the two. People will do almost anything for glory in what is often a neurotic compulsion. But they will not do as much, if anything, for naked power itself. And from glory to idolatry there is but one small step, which in history has often been taken.

With this historical sketch in mind, it is important to recognize

that in the modern situation, particularly in that of advanced industrial society, the Cult of the Aesthetic takes precedence over the
Cult of the Present and the Cult of the Quantum. This is because it
provides the most effective practical synthesis between the Consumer Style and the Objective Style. Such as synthesis serves the
interests of corporate power in numerous ways, including not only
that of glorifying such power but of giving it more effective control
over the masses. This synthesis can be best understood by recognizing the dialectical relationship between the Objective Style and the
Consumer Style. The dialectic is evident in the fact that the Objective Style is characterized by detachment while the Consumer Style
is characterized by identification. And yet each style complements
the other. In other words, the scientist stands back and looks at the
object from the stance of a spectator; the consumer, if he is to buy
the object, must identify with it. The salesman sees the complementary character of both attitudes and uses the detached knowledge
of the one to secure the identification of the other. The detachment
and identification as opposites have a unity in the complementary
use which is made of them. In particular, this complementary use is
best served by the objective use of imagery which secures the
identification of the consumer with the product. In this respect, Truth
as the technical use of imagery is the means of conditioning the
consumer to buy almost automatically. For this purpose the image
must be made attractive, whether it be that of the package on the
shelf or of the picture of the product in a magazine. It must also be
placed upon an attractive background such as nature unspoiled,
beautiful homes and gardens, and festive occasions. The same
technique pertains to the "selling" of political candidates to the
electorate, corporate power to the public, and of clergy to a
congregation. An effective image is essential.

All of this suggests that those dedicated to the Way and Truth
of corporate power will increase their skill in the use of imagery.
They will produce a new breed of artists. Indeed, the demand for
the service of such artists will probably increase as success contributes to greater expectations, or as failure dims success and creates
a nostalgia for once enlarged expectations. Out of it all will undoubtedly emerge the preeminence of the Cult of the Aesthetic
which will encourage a new positive form of idolatry for the promo-

tion of power. For a mass society of lonely individuals the appeal of such a cult with its positive idolatry, in whatever form, could be virtually irresistible. It could involve an aura of glory which could heighten the Cult of the Aesthetic to a hypnotic level of fascination.

5.
the invisible sin

The real sin of advanced industrial society is invisible sin, corresponding to its invisible religion. Such sin is closely related to the peculiar power of such a society and the secrecy with which it operates. This means that it is especially related to the science, technology, and technique which facilitate such power and secrecy. As a result it enters into the structure and operation of advanced industrial society, its technopolitan character and culture, and control of its people, including their lifestyle, character, and consciousness. It enters into what is basic to such a society and the progress which qualifies it as industrial in the advanced sense of the term. This suggests why the major forms of such invisible sin are seldom if ever recognized by traditional religious authorities for inclusion within their catalogue of sins. It also suggests why the same forms of invisible sins are never recognized by legal authorities for inclusion within their category of offences against society and the individual. Indeed, most religious and legal authorities, and the public at large, would likely consider the major forms of invisible sin as the positive, progressive, and essential conditions by which industry and civilization have reached their unprecedented height of achievement.

There have always been the common variety of invisible sin in any society and individual—the unconfessed, unacknowledged, concealed, and even repressed sin. There have always been the subtler forms of invisible sin within the context of law and accepted protocol, such as stealing within the law, lying within the truth, hating within the holy, and insulting within the courteous. None of these are new or peculiar to advanced industrial society. They are as old as man himself and his various civilizations.

But the major forms of invisible sin which have emerged in advanced industrial society are to a large extent new and unprecedented. This is because they are correlated with the science, technology, and technique which are so highly definitive of such society. As a result they do not resemble the older and more common forms of invisible sin but are deeper and more concealed in their invisibility. They are not only concealed by complexity, efficiency, and an extraordinary emphasis upon the positive and the aesthetic, but by such correlated factors as a new emphasis on community, status, and satisfaction. As a result the hidden amorality common to all the major forms of such invisible sin which generally pervades advanced industrial society is scarcely recognized.

It is now appropriate in the light of these preliminary observations to outline the three major forms of such invisible sin which will be examined in the present chapter. This will include their biblical parallels in spite of the fact that they are, to a large extent, new and unprecedented. Yet it is one of the peculiarities of biblical insight into sin that it often has an uncanny awareness of the problem with a surprising relevance to any era or type of society.

The three major forms of invisible sin in advanced industrial society are respectively concealed within the three major styles of life. As a convenient outline of the procedure which will be used to examine them, including the biblical parallels, the following has been adopted.

1. *Discontinuity* is the invisible sin implicit in the Consumer Style —a sin parallel to the First Temptation in the Gospel of Matthew, ch. 4, verses 1–4.

2. *Reductionism* is the invisible sin implicit in the Objective Style —a sin parallel to the Second Temptation in the Gospel of Matthew, ch. 4, verses 5–7.

3. *Idolization* is the invisible sin implicit in the Aesthetic Style—a sin parallel to the Third Temptation in the Gospel of Matthew, ch. 4, verses 8–10.

At this stage it should be further indicated that the use of the biblical parallels from Matthew 4:1–10 is influenced by the use which Dostoevsky made of them in his penetrating interpretation of the three temptations of Jesus in *The Brothers Karamazov.*[1] His interpretation at least suggested a peculiar similarity between the invisible sin in each of the three styles of life (Consumer, Objective, Aesthetic) and the respective temptations of Jesus by the Devil. In other words, Matthew 4:1–10 seems to be a penetrating and highly relevant interpretation of the temptations of advanced industrial society. In this case the Grand Inquisitor (the Devil) would not be represented by the Spanish cardinal but probably by some Mephistopholian scientist, engineer, or technomaniac who, with all the apparent humanitarianism and piety assumed by the Devil and the promise of power and glory made by him, would be much more representative.

Discontinuity as the Invisible Sin of the Consumer Style

The invisible sin of discontinuity implicit in the Consumer Style is closely related to the Cult of the Present. This is because of the strong emphasis which the Consumer Style puts upon buying in the present and of not clinging to past commodities or postponing their purchase till the future. As a result of this emphasis on buying in the present, the break with the past and the future is appropriately described as *commodity discontinuity.* This kind of economic discontinuity is promoted by an artificially manipulated downgrading of commodities bought in the recent past, as if they were old, antiquated and out-of-date in a surprisingly short period of time. A similar manipulation involves built-in obsolescence of commodities so they will wear out more quickly, the deliberate changing of models and styles, and the contrived scarcity of parts so that new equipment will have to be purchased. In such downgrading of the past there is a hidden, greedy, extravagant, unnecessary production of waste in the name of profit, the ultimate result of which is a depletion of valuable natural resources.

Along similar lines there is a downgrading of the future for which the consumer is urged not to repair, postpone, or save. The emphasis is upon buying and consuming now with little or no thought of tommorrow. The whole trend is promoted by a vast range and variety of innovation which science, technology, and technique made possible for big industry. This affects almost everything that is bought, used, and consumed. In this respect the consumer is caught and exploited—a fact generally hidden from him by his affluence so that the Cult of the Present seems highly positive and prestigious. This is reenforced by the euphoria of satisfaction with which he believes in the human quality of his style of life, even though in a hidden manner it is dehumanizing.

Not only is he unable to see such dehumanizing, but he is unable to see how the same downgrading of the past and future is a downgrading of history and hope, a downgrading of the unchangeable and eternal, a downgrading of law and personal identity with each of the latter (law and identity) presupposing continuity. He cannot see the evil which business promotes in its pressure to live the Consumer Style. He cannot see how in an implicitly atheistic and godless manner it strikes at the basic faith of the three forms of traditional religion in their affirmation of historical, legal, and apostolic continuity with the past and their affirmation of evangelic, messianic hope which involves continuity with the future. At the same time public morality suffers from the same discontinuity because moral standards and norms which presuppose continuity are fragmented and eroded. This in turn promotes anomic behavior such as crime.[2,3]

To this point the focus has been upon commodity discontinuity. But if space permitted, much the same could be said of the negative effects of related forms of discontinuity, such as generational, residential, and occupational discontinuity. Much could also be said of the kind of logical discontinuity which the implosive impact of television has upon the linear, logical character of the print medium. At this point the extent to which traditional religion is a religion of the book and therefore dependent on the linear character of the print medium, and so also upon this kind of continuity, only emphasizes another aspect of the way in which it is threatened by discontinuity.[4]

As an illustration of the magnitude of the inherent danger and sin that can be identified with discontinuity, Gunther Anders' "Reflections on the H Bomb" is most enlightening.[5] Assuming that the bomb has been exploded, he then analyzes why no one accepts any responsibility for the consequences. He puts the main point this way: "The chain of events leading up to the explosion is composed of so many links, the process has involved so many different agencies, so many intermediate steps and partial actions, none of which is the crucial one, that in the end no one can be regarded as the agent. Everyone has a good conscience, because no conscience is required at any point." In other words, the many links, the different agencies, the intermediate steps, and partial actions are together definitive of a discontinuity which prevents anyone from seeing the total process, except perhaps a few at the top whose comprehension is itself largely indirect (another form of discontinuity).

Anders then goes on to say that "the specialized worker is not conscious of the fact that the conscientious efforts of a number of specialists can add up to the most monstrous lack of conscience: just as any other industrial enterprise he has no insight into the process as a whole. . . . And yet it may result in the death of all mankind." At this point it is appropriate to add that such can be the awful consequence of the discontinuity to which specialization can contribute.

Discontinuity and the First Temptation (Matthew 4:1–4)

At this point the parallel between discontinuity as the invisible sin of the Consumer Style of Life and the First Temptation with which the Devil confronted Jesus in the Wilderness should be recognized. The discontinuity concerns the emphasis upon massive consumption of commodities in the present, which in the connotation of the Invisible Religion means the Cult of the Present.

What the Devil asks amounts to a similar discontinuity with the past, in which amazing abundance would break the continuity of poverty and scarcity from which the vast majority of people had suffered. It would also break the likely continuity of poverty and scarcity with the future. What the Devil wants, he wants now as evidence of power—the kind of power which he thinks Jesus should have as proof of any claim to messiahship. The Devil asks that Jesus change the stones into bread as miraculous proof of his messianic power and therefore proof of that promised abundance which would be divinely generated by the coming of the Kingdom of God on earth as the ancient apocalyptic hope had visualized it.[6] The Devil is very positive and seemingly humanitarian. He wants a miracle of production, in fact, the equivalent of mass production as proof of messianic identity. If he were God he would first solve the economic problem. He would transform the desert places of the earth into gardens of plenty.

The Devil's request to turn stones into bread, undoubtedly on a massive scale consistent with his posture as a humanitarian, is no more extravagant than the ambitions of advanced industrial society. Metaphorically speaking, the industrial power of such society turns billions of stones into bread in what has been visualized as an approaching era of automated abundance. As the fulfillment of the positive appeal of the Devil as practical proof of down-to-earth divinity, this signifies unlimited prosperity, unlimited economic growth, and an unlimited gross national product. As evidence of discontinuity with the past and future as would also be true of the discontinuity of the Devil's desire for a comparable miracle of production, commodity discontinuity would undoubtedly be accompanied by other forms. As Anders has shown in his analysis of the production of the hydrogen bomb, specialization can produce its own form of discontinuity with horrendous results.

If the invisible sin in such a consumer society is not already evident, it is clearly implied in the answer which Jesus gives to the Devil (as he gives to modern corporate power which so obviously promotes such a society). "Man shall not live by bread alone but by every word that proceeds from the mouth of God." Jesus recognized, of course, that the poor and needy must be fed, that man must have bread to eat in order to live. This was elemental. But the point he stressed was that such consuming must not become an end in itself, and therefore the changing of stones into bread must not become an end in itself. The point which he stressed is evident in the phrase "not by bread alone." Automated abundance and unlimited economic expansion are not the ultimate solution to the human problem. Prosperity is not the final answer to man's deepest need. Indeed, to wallow in wealth without working and to exploit the resources of the earth without responsibility is in the end self-destructive. Man is such in his nature that he must be saved from himself whether he be rich or poor, individual or corporate in power. He must be saved from falsely absolutizing his dedication to consuming and producing as if such power were his God. Such false absolutizing is the equivalent of the Devil—invisible and concealed under the miracle of achievement and positive satisfaction. This is why man must hear "every word that proceeds from the mouth of God."

Reductionism as the Invisible Sin of the Objective Style

The invisible sin of reductionism implicit in the Objective Style is closely related to the Cult of the Quantum. This is because of the strong emphasis which the Objective Style puts upon quantification. The concept of quantification includes a wide range and variety of examples. Beginning with the more obvious example of measurement, along with theories and forms of measurement, and equipment for measurement (including weighing scales, clocks and watches, computers, and data banks), it is obvious that measurement alone is a basic and universal necessity of advanced industrial society. Production and merchandising would be impossible without it. Beyond the range and variety and the equipment for measurement, the emphasis on quantification involves a large number of professions. Merely naming them will suggest the extent to which quantification has entered into the life and work of society and the individual. There are bankers, accountants, statisticians, data processors, surveyors, draftsmen, weighers, packagers, check-out clerks, engineers, production managers, and many others—all concerned with quantities and quantification. The commonest question of advanced industrial society is the question "how much?" which is widely used for the valuation of the individual as illustrated by the question, "How much is he worth?" It as if the amount of money, stocks, bonds, or real estate he possessed were the principal measure of personal worth. Little wonder that such an emphasis is placed upon profit, dividends, market indices, exchange rates, numbers of jobs, and the gross national production in what amounts to a grand finale of quantification.

Quantification as the most obvious and widespread form of reductionism is closely related to other forms. Together they tend to coalesce into a web of reductionism which has a tremendous impact upon society and the individual and upon the natural order itself. The term reductionism has reference to any way in which the vertical (height and depth) dimension of human and natural life are reduced both downwards and upwards to the middle level of the neutral. In every instance it means that in some sense quality is reduced to quantity, as if the only reality were the measurable. In respect to nature it means the disenchantment or desacralization of nature from something beautiful, mysterious, and refreshing into something neutral, which for this reason is at once amenable to exploitation and plunder. In this respect nature is reduced to a thing. Any part of nature which is especially beautiful has to be protected by law from the quantitative plunderers, in what becomes a public park. In respect to the individual, the heights of his aspiration of spirit and the depths of his intuition of mind are reduced from above downwards and from below upwards to a middle level of the neutral, at which he virtually becomes an automation.

Closely associated with this reductionism, which is equivalent to his depersonalization, is a comparable form of reductionism which is equivalent to the neturalizing of his moral imperative or conscience in its best and most legitimate sense. This means the reduction of the imperative downwards to the middle, neutral level of the indicative, in what amounts to the disappearance of the "ought" into the "is" and a resultant causalistic amorality. In this respect the individual is further automatized by loss of conscience.

Expressed in biblical terminology, reductionism involves this same loss of conscience or loss of soul. But even more important biblical examples include the reduction of the three-tiered conception of the cosmos to the middle neutral level. The reduction of heaven downwards and hell upwards causes both to become non-existent in terms of the neutral middle level of a secularized earth —all of which is atheism. In more general terms this means the reduction of divine transcendence downwards and the reduction of the same transcendence (immanence) upwards to the same neutral middle level of a secularized earth—which simply means there is no God beyond and no God within, which again is atheism. This as invisible sin is kept strictly hidden within the Cult of the Quantum with its emphasis on quantification and techniques.

It is understandable how reductionism in its many forms, including amorality and automatism, conditions society and the life and conduct of the individual. Life in a large city, adaptation to bureaucracy, and obedience to a multiplicity of regulations and techniques has this effect. In effect the individual is conditioned psychologically like an experimental rat running a maze—a fact which the "rat race" idiom at once reveals. Translated into the immediate situation, this means driving in horrendous traffic, obeying the signals, mechanical regularity at work, obedience to instructions, following the program, and never questioning the source or destination of any order. As an expression of the dedicated conversion of the individual as an "other-directed," "organization" man it means the type of conduct which is essentially amoral.

As an indication of the serious implications of such amorality when it has reached the stage of automation, Louis Mumford's observations are illuminating in the way in which they focus on the danger to which it leads.

> Ultimately organization man has no reason except as a de-personalized servo-mechanism in the mega-machine. On these terms Adolf Eichmann, the obedient exterminator who carried out Hitler's orders with unswerving fidelity, should be hailed as the hero of our time. But, unfortunately our time has produced many such heroes who have been willing to do at a safe distance with napalm or atom bombs by a mere press of the release button what the exterminators of Belsen and Auschwitz did by old fashioned handcraft methods. . . . In every country there are now countless Eichmanns in administration offices and business corporations, in universities, in laboratories, in the armed forces, orderly, obedient people ready to carry out officially sanctioned fantasy however de-humanized and debased.[7]

The problem in Mumford's examples is not one which can be understood by means of simplistic moral judgment. All of them are examples of those who believe in what they are doing, who sincerely carry out orders, and who have what may be called innocent feelings which accompany the unrecognized and therefore invisible amorality. Indeed, they may be impeccable gentlemen who hold high positions in churches and religious organizations and on governing boards of colleges and universities. In their private family life, as was shown in the case of the Nazi death camp exterminators, they may be good parents and respected neighbors. The positive influence of the church (which more often comforts than challenges them) and the emphasis on the human side of management do not cope with or even recognize the invisible sin, which devotees of the invisible religion fail to see themselves.[8]

Reductionism and the Second Temptation (Matthew 4: 5–7)

At this point the parallel between reductionism as the invisible sin of the Objective Style of Life and the Second Temptation with which the Devil confronted Jesus in the wilderness (Matt. 4: 5–7) should be recognized. The Devil asks Jesus to provide a further proof of messianic power and the coming of the kingdom—a pragmatic objective demonstration which would leave no one in doubt. He asks him to leap from the pinnacle of the temple and instead of crashing to his death to be borne up miraculously by angelic hands. In this way, according to the Devil, he would provide visible proof of his identity, presumably in the presence of a vast crowd of people which often gathered in the temple court below. At the same time, in keeping with the humanitarian role which he adopted in the first temptation, the Devil adopts a similarly positive role in this temptation—a pious one who quotes Scripture in support of what he requests Jesus to do (verse 6). What the Devil expects is that the power of God will be put to the same test as the modern laboratory provides. It is to be authenticated by experimental demonstration and therefore to be considered as belonging to the same objective order as science, technology, and technique. Jesus is being asked to adopt the Objective Style in response to what the Devil regarded as the criterion of truth, with the emphasis shifted in the direction of power. At this point the Devil is obviously resorting to pragmatic reductionism.

But again the invisible sin in such a style is indicated in the answer given to the devil. "You shall not tempt the Lord your God." God shall not be put to the test which the laboratory provides, as if man had in such a test a measuring stick of God—as if the power symbolized by the laboratory were his god, his ultimate authority, his final pragmatic proof, with God himself the victim of reductionism —indeed a quantum.

Vacuity: The Combined Sin of Discontinuity and Reductionism

Before considering the major form of invisible sin in the Positive Style of Life and its closely correlated Cult of the Aesthetic, it is important to recognize the more radical form of invisible sin to which discontinuity and reductionism contribute in their combined effect. To put this in a few words, the one erodes and destroys the normative in the horizontal dimension (past-present-future); the other erodes and destroys the normative in the vertical dimension (height, middle, depth). Theoretically all that is left of the individual is the minimal identity symbolized by the intersection of the two dimensions, which is merely a point or dot. Keeping in mind the dynamism of the field of forces in which he lives and works, this means that his existence tends to resemble that of a particle out of orbit which moves in various directions in an unpredictable manner.

As one whose typology is characterized by such normlessness and minimal identity, it means that he has paid the price of openness to all the persuaders, promoters, manipulators, developers, and the various media. Their power has meant a canopic message of social change which has come in upon him from every direction and upon the value and belief systems by which he has lived. His openness has been changed to emptiness. As a normless, selfless man he has become an empty man. His conversion to an other-directed openness has resulted in such emptiness. This amounts to a depletion of the self comparable to the depletion of nature due to a similar exploitation of its resources. His openness is an invitation to the exploitation of the physical resources of the self on the personality market, which like the exploitation of nature likewise leads to emptiness.

The truth is that man is being abolished as a person. Science technology and technique in the service of corporate power especially in advanced industrial society is emptying him of any significance. As one who is unique, who is qualified by a peculiar centeredness, out of which arises a corresponding creativity, he is being emptied, conditioned, and explained away. He is being reduced to a complex of function. His person and personality are being conceived as illusory. His freedom is being conceived as an

interplay of forces; his experience of purpose as a deceptive fan-
tasy. He is regarded as devoid of transcendence, even of self-
transcendence, which when so described is minimized as only a
difference of quality capable of being reduced to quantity. He is
not regarded as possessing inherent rights, which have been previously described as the rights of man. The increasing assumption is
that he comes out of nothingness, lives and moves and has his being
in nothingness, and returns to nothingness. In strict conformity to this
conception of him, he cannot generate meaning out of himself, when
there is no meaning (or self-transcendence) there to begin with. He
cannot generate anything out of himself except an illusion called
meaning and therefore cannot overcome nothingness. His motivation is not inherently teleological but only an impression of pure
causality.

As described, the problem pertains to the post-romantic, post-
existential, post-industrial world in which man has completely seen
through himself—his motives, thoughts, feelings, actions, identity,
creativity, and transcendence—in the same way in which he has
seen through his law, custom, tradition, morality, religion, and ideology. Even his so-called real or authentic self, which many would like
to exempt from this fate, is included in this emptying process. The
problem is beyond the intellectual and psychological because the
scientific and technological environment is structured in such a way
that it envelops and implodes him so that he has little or no means
of escape. Even if he yields to the adoration of corporate power
and becomes converted in the most positive sense to such power,
it does not mean that he is any less an automation or empty man.

Much has been written of this peculiar normlessness, selfless-
ness, and emptiness by therapists, sociologists, dramatists, novelists,
philosophers, and others. They have generally regarded it as a
characteristic of a rapidly developing urbanized, industrialized society in which the acceleration and multidimensional forms of change
have this effect upon the human being. It is a complex, enigmatic
condition, as suggested by the variety of synonyms used to signify
what it means. It is often described as meaninglessness, which of
course is partially true. But its paralyzing numbness, disorientation,
and anxiety make it anything but meaningless. It is often described
as loneliness, which is also true, but it is a peculiar, debilitating

loneliness which is quite different from the restful character of normal solitude. It has been described as a feeling of insignificance and powerlessness, which again, while true, is an implicit comparison presupposing a particular milieu. It has been more poignantly and generally described as a loss of nerve, a tedium vitae, and a malaise which can readily reach the suicidal point of a loss of a will to live. Nevertheless, in all of these experiences there is a minimal identity which remains and by which the experiences are possible.[9,10,11,12]

At the same time there are often ambiguities as illustrated in the synonym of emptiness, which by its very nature signifies a vacuum. Obviously a vacuum tends to suck things into itself, and to this extent it symbolizes the tendency of the empty individual to suck "things" into himself indiscriminately from his social environment—a little of this, a little of that, in what amounts to a conglomeration.[13] On the other hand, the empty individual, unlike a vacuum, is often volatile inasmuch as his normlessness permits the release of detached psychical energy. For this reason he tends to be explosive, unpredictable, and prone to violence and crime, and therefore easily attracted to gangs, extremists, and mass movements.

Implicit in all forms of the condition, regardless of the synonym, is always a greater or lesser degree of estrangement or alienation. This appears, for example, in the way in which apathy or loss of interest and motivation can exemplify the typical ambiguity of the condition and explode into hatred and often violence. In effect, the apathy (like the other forms such as emptiness, insignificance, and powerlessness) is like a smouldering fire which can burst into flame. Surprisingly enough, one of the recently recognized factors contributing to alienation is the gap between expectations and reality, especially in a society in which affluence and innovation abound. As the gap expands out of proportion to what can be reasonably expected, even at a high level of affluence (Consumer Style) and technological innovation (Objective Style), alienation expands accordingly. As a special form of discontinuity it contributes a surprisingly large proportion of alienation.

In addition to the synonyms already used to describe this complex, enigmatic condition is one which enters into all of them in a rather hidden, unrecognized manner. All of them in one way or another are really forms of nothingness. As another synonym, this one in its literal meaning as "no-thing-ness" at once suggests why the condition cannot be described and therefore particularized. As "no-thing-ness" it is not an object of thought or perception which can be grasped by the mind or observed. It cannot be specified as an act of sin, as a transgression against law or even as an omission of what ought to have been done in terms of law. It is rather the fading away of law as the normative—its disappearance—including even the disappearance of conscience in such a way as not to be noticed. It does so quietly and nonspecifically in what is a typically canopic, gestaltic form as a function of social change, particularly in the two primary dimensions of discontinuity and reductionism. 14,15,16,17,18

As invisible sin it is not confessed and not the subject of repentance. As nonspecific and indeterminate it is not perceived for what it really is by traditional religion. As a result, the ways of coping with it are varied and generally unintended for such a purpose, except to arouse more interest and generate a more dynamic form of traditional religion. As such, power is considered the answer, especially positive power. So it is assumed that what is needed is more fellowship and friendship, more fun and festivity, more discussion and renewal conferences, more committees and sub-committees, more organization and planning, more mergers and unions, more retreats and sectarian separation, more charismatic and ecstatic experience—none of which get at the root of the invisible sin or the sources of power and the canopic, gestaltic change which are producing it.

Idolization as the Invisible Sin of the Positive Style

The invisible sin of idolization implicit in the Positive Style is closely related to the Cult of the Aesthetic. To understand such idolization, it is necessary to remember not only that the Positive Style is common to the Consumer and Objective Styles, but that the Cult of the Aesthetic is common to the Cult of the Present and the Cult of the Quantum. If this latter claim is not clear, it must be remembered that the Cult of the Present requires the aesthetic for the consumer to identify quickly in the present with any given product; the Cult of the Quantum requires the aesthetic for the technician and operator to be attracted by the power which the quantum signifies. It concerns the affinity between the power of beauty and the beauty of power, in which the former is invariably used to promote the latter.

This was emphasized in the previous chapter as a typical means by which powerful aristocracies throughout history have enhanced their power, especially as a means of securing the identification and loyalty of their people. They promoted what was virtually a Cult of the Aesthetic in all their emphasis on color, ritual, pomp, and protocol and majestic titles in the direction of virtual deification. All of this was promoted in the context of the architectural splendor of palaces and cathedrals. At times the heads of state like the Pharoahs and the Caesars were actually worshiped.

In recognizing how the aesthetic has been used throughout history as a means of social control and manipulation, it should be also recognized how its use for the same purpose has now proliferated. While it is less associated with the old aristocracies which have largely declined, it has been appropriated by the great corporate sources of power and greatly expanded and specialized. It has reached the point of an extravaganza of promotionalism in what could be called *technaestheticism*. In effect, the Cult of the Aesthetic and technology have combined. This was implied in the reference earlier to the emergence of a new breed of artists synonymous with engineers of imagery.

Their range and variety of skill and influence has been enormously magnified by what has been called the visual revolution, which has produced what to a large extent is a visual culture. Photography, motion pictures, television, professional sports (with its vast arenas, stadiums, and grandstands), as well as tourism have provided the means by which technaestheticism flourishes. In what was said earlier about the dialectical relationship between the Objective and the Consumer Styles, the former with its detachment securing the identification of the latter, both styles with their respective cults have a close connection with technaestheticism. What the buyer consumes now (present) must as a quantum (commodity) have aesthetic appeal. It must have a good image in the context of the new visual culture. This, of course, means that the "technaesthetes," if such a word may be used, are of many kinds—packagers, designers, advertisers, architects, salesmen, window dressers, and public relations experts. As a result, almost every prominent individual and business firm is concerned about its public image. The image must be highly positive with strong aesthetic appeal. The same applies to any product (quantum) such as an automobile, a piece of furniture, a dress, or a suit of clothes. In every instance the purpose is to sell, develop euphoria in the customer, and secure his loyalty so that he virtually finds his soul in the image. The same pertains to personality. Technaesthetes include politicians who are processed through political beauty parlors to improve their image. They also include the category of stars in what is now a world of stardom. There are more stars, hockey, baseball, and football stars, political stars, and what was perhaps the earliest example, evangelistic stars in the field of religious revivalism. In this context it is understandable why in recent years there was a movie and theatrical production called *Jesus Christ, Superstar.*

The invisible sin implicit in the Cult of the Aesthetic and its technaestheticism is of several kinds. The first concerns the identification of the consumer and the employee of an organization or corporate power with its image, and indeed with itself, in such a way that they converted to it and therefore to its invisible religion. As this theme of conversion was developed in chapter three, it had so many of the characteristics of a genuine religious conversion—in this instance to the invisible religion of corporate power. In this form of conversion the image of corporate power was an important factor in the conversion. The individual identified not only with the power or organization but with the image in a manner which tended to comprehend the whole of his life. In this respect the invisible sin was idolization or idolatry. To a lesser extent, as any individual tends to find his soul in a commodity—in his automobile or his television set or in certain prized and coveted artifacts—he exhibits a similar idolization. This, of course, is encouraged by the professional persuaders who urge people to buy and who play up the beauty, the style and prestige of the commodities they promote.

The second form of invisible sin implicit in the Cult of the Aesthetic, again under the category of idolization, is the way in which the consumer like the citizen throughout history has been manipulated by the ruling class by means of the aesthetic. This need not be further elaborated except to say that political and military power in the present world have developed their technaestheticism for this purpose to an unprecedented extent, assisted where necessary by the new media at their disposal. The emergence of the totalitarian state in its various forms has been another powerful influence which has magnified this type of manipulation of its citizens.

The third form of invisible sin implicit in the Cult of the Aesthetic, again under the category of idolization, is the way in which the aesthetic, including its imagery, has been used to conceal the invisible sin of discontinuity and reductionism. This pertains more especially to their combined effect, which has already been described at length in the section titled: "Vacuity: The Combined Sin of Discontinuity and Reductionism." The aesthetic and its accompanying imagery conceals such vacuity in a most effective manner. This follows from the peculiar way in which the power of beauty serves the beauty of power. Since the power of beauty serves power, it serves at the same time to conceal the vacuity which power produces and indeed promotes.

As already indicated, there is a point beyond which power is no longer bound by laws and norms. It not only attains such magnitude that it makes its own laws and norms in a protean manner, but it also erodes accepted, traditional laws and norms. This has been evident enough in the way in which discontinuity and reductionism operate as expressions of power. Both contribute to vacuity, which, if exposed, would be frightening if not terrifying to behold. But there is more to it than this. In a sense, power of such magnitude welcomes vacuity as a peculiar kind of space in which it can operate without being restricted by norms, laws, standards, values, and the like. By concealing vacuity in this respect, namely as the operating space welcomed by power, the aesthetic with its imagery serve a double purpose. It not only conceals the frightening and terrifying (*horror vacui*) from the public and even from power itself, but it promotes the operation of power in such vacuity. In this respect the aesthetic and particularly its imagery (or indeed its image, if the corporate power be total and dictatorial) is in a double sense of the term literally idolization or idolatry. It is beautiful but inwardly empty, a kind of encapsulated emptiness, solely in the service of power and therefore an idol in the biblical sense of the term.

Idolization and the Third Temptation (Matthew 4:8–10)

At this point it is appropriate to consider the the parallel between such idolization and the Third Temptation (Matthew 4:8–10)
with which the Devil confronted Jesus in the wilderness. This can be
considered more briefly than the two previous parallels with the
temptations. The devil takes Jesus up to a high mountain and shows
him all the kingdoms of the world and the glory of them. Then he
says, "All of these I will give you, if you will fall down and worship
me." This is the temptation of unlimited world power—the temptation of world domination—which has been the temptation of nations, empires, churches and, other organizations throughout
history. It is the temptation of modern superpowers, modern defense
departments with their earth-encircling armies, navies, and air
forces, and modern multi-national corporations. The glory of them
is the aesthetic appeal of such power which confers a god-like pride
(hubris) upon the possessors in what amounts to an expensive fan-
tasy. Their assumption is that they have brought the best order of
society into existence by their power—their equivalent of utopia.
In depicting this third temptation, the glory even more than the
power defines the Positive Style. And such glory is aesthetic and
dramatic. It satisfies the desire to dominate and symbolizes the
greatest possible success. But the condition which the Devil imposes
is one which exposes the focus of worship and the invisible sin of
idolization. It is the condition of falling down and worshiping him
in what amounts to the essence of idolization—the Devil as the idol,
the Chief Idol—in what may be recognized as Devil Worship, which
all idolization tends to be in the end.[19] Thus the reply which sharply
counters such idolization is the forthright biblical imperative "You
shall worship the Lord your God and him only shall you serve." The
emphasis on the adverb *only* clearly excludes the worship of power
and the "power god." Such in the end is really the worship of the
devil, however concealed it may be under the positive, aesthetic
imagery of the invisible religion.[20]

6.
the sovereignty
of the invisible religion

The Strange Contribution of the Judeo-Christian Religion

In view of the various respects considered in the previous chapters in which the Judeo-Christian religion tends to be infiltrated and captivated by the Invisible Religion of Corporate Power, it is important to recognize that the Judeo-Christian religion is particularly susceptible to such a consequence. At various times throughout its history the Judeo-Christian religion has contributed in strange ways to its own captivity and therefore to the sovereignty of the Invisible Religion of Corporate Power. This seems to have had much to do with the fact that the Judeo-Christian religion itself is a religion of power. Its God is characterized as dynamic and as one who is omnipotent and who therefore has all power in heaven and earth and who has created the universe. Indeed, his people throughout their history, century after century, have always regarded him as a God who acted and have trusted and prayed to him as a God of power who answered their prayers. This is the very opposite of a god who is static, and more of an ideal or example to emulate. It is the very opposite of the mystical, which as such is without any evidence of action or power in heaven and earth.

In emphasizing that the God of the Judeo-Christian religion is a God of Power, it can be further stated that throughout their long history its people have therefore always been susceptible to a pecular *temptation.* In various ways they could possess such power to secure advantages for themselves and promote their own interests. In this temptation the emphasis has often been upon God giving or endowing them with his power or upon acting in and through them as his servants for this purpose.

Several examples of this temptation may be cited in order to indicate its subtlety and how readily it has been used to promote the sovereignty of the Invisible Religion of Corporate Power and unwittingly the captivity of those who yielded to such temptation. Various kings in the history of Israel tended to assume absolute authority after the manner of oriental despots. As those whose power was given them under God and who ruled and served their people in his name, a certain aura of holiness tended to be appropriated by them. At the same time, a certain authoritarianism crept into their policy and practice under which their people were restive and oppressed. On occasion this became so critical that the whole problem became even more of a religious than a political problem, as certain of the prophets readily recognized. A similar temptation has been evident at times in the history of Christian kings and emperors in Europe. A similar aura of holiness has been appropriated by them and a similar authoritarianism evident in their policy and practice. As an illustration of what this signified, perhaps the doctrine of the "divine right of kings" and all of its consequences is one of the best examples. This was a doctrine which in effect appropriated the power of God as a means of royal administration and therefore enhanced the sovereignty of the Invisible Religion of Power for the reigning monarch.

Another example, both in the history of Hebraism and Christianity, has been the tendency to interpret the doctrine of election and predestination as a form of divine favoritism in the interest of promoting nationalism. This was a powerful factor in perverting monotheism into a form of monopolism. On the assumption of being the chosen people of God, and therefore as his favorites, he was expected to give them of his power and bless them with success as he would no other people. This was not necessarily overt and seldom official, but it operated subliminally as a powerful temptation. The prophet Amos had this temptation in mind when he warned his people in the name of God: "You only have I known of all the families of the earth: therefore I will punish you for all your iniquities" (Amos 3:2).

Another example concerns the priests and their possession of divine power, which has been interpreted as a peculiar endowment by virtue of their ordination and status in the hierarchy of authority. As those who were therefore regarded as potentiated with holy power, with perhaps a similar potentiation of their office, the collective religious and political influence of their policy and practice has been more or less equal to that of kings or an aristocracy. It was certainly this in the case of the ancient Sadducean priestly aristocracy in Jerusalem, which was generally wealthy. In the history of the Christian church there have been a variety of examples of a similar priestly claim to the possession and monopoly of divine power in the name of such holiness. In each instance the collective influence has been both religious and political, which at times has led to critical situations involving power struggles, oppression, reaction, rebellion, and bloodshed. Among the noteworthy examples have been the Roman Catholic Curia and its equivalent in the Eastern Orthodox churches as well as in various state churches in Western Europe and Britain. In differing degrees the various Protestant churches have had a similar presupposition on the part of their clerical elites on the possession and administration of divine power in the exercise of their authority.

Another example has been the misuse of divine law throughout the long history of Hebraism and Christianity in what has been generally known as *legalism,* and which in turn overlooks the biblical emphasis on the law as the power of God and not primarily statutes and principles. Such legalism has assumed various forms, such as modes of expiation by which sin is presumably removed; the modes of meriting divine favor and securing increased credit in the "heavenly ledger"; the modes of ascetic self-punishment and discipline and even suffering for which a similar credit is presumably obtained in the heavenly ledger; and finally the recent techniques applied to organization, worship, evangelism, education, and pastoral care as new forms of legalism by which divine power is presumably more efficiently administered and for which heavenly credit is also received.

The subtle implication in all these forms of legalism is two-fold. *First,* it is implied that the law which as divine power is higher than God is such that God is obliged to obey it in crediting merit in the "heavenly ledger." *Second,* such law is always more or less defined in its particulars by those who presume to use it in these various ways for their own advantage (power). In these respects they have transformed it into an idol, and the merit supposedly credited to them in their "heavenly ledger" into a projection of their self-evaluation and power and all the more into an idol. As a more extreme example of legalism, if the law of God is equated with the mores (power) of the business world and seen as both anterior and posterior to the gospel, two conclusions follow. As anterior to the gospel it defines what types of wrong conduct violate the business mores (power) and from which Christ therefore saves the individual. As posterior to the gospel it defines what types of right conduct fulfil the business mores (power) and for which Christ saves the individual. In other words, Christ is a servant of the business mores (power), and both he and the mores are jointly idols.

This whole conception of legalism (power) which focuses on Christ as a servant of the business mores largely explains the extent and manner by which the various denominations are correlated with the class structure. This includes the extent to which their life, work, worship, and faith (cf. chapters 2–5) are modified by the degree of success (power) and failure (powerlessness) found at any specific class level.[1,2] For this reason missionary outreach is to a surprising extent to the poor and unsuccessful (down-and-outs) rather than to the rich, the successful, and the elite—to East Harlem rather than to Wall Street, to the ghettos rather than to suburbia, to alcoholics and beggars rather than to the directors of multi-national corporations. This is no reflection on the social and religious concern for the poor, the unsuccessful, and the outcasts, nor upon the generous and practical aid provided them. It is rather a reflection on the failure to see the hidden need of the rich, the successful, and the elite which may be as great or even greater than their opposites.

Another example of the temptation to which the Judeo-Christian religion is particularly susceptible is a certain misinterpretation of the doctrine of creation—again, more or less subliminal. This is the

sacraments and excommunication. For Martin Luther this amounted
to what he described as the *Babylonian Captivity of the Church.*

But there was another form of captivity which went back in
history as far as Constantine the Great and which has continued
through Catholicism and Protestantism down to the present day. This
is a form of captivity which has received little if any serious attention
by the churches or by its leading theologians. It is the captivity which
is represented by the *militarization of the cross of Christ.* One of
the earliest indications of this kind of captivity was the adoption of
the cross by Constantine himself as a military symbol, with the
slogan that "in this sign we conquer."[4,5] In later centuries, notably
in the eleventh, twelfth, and thirteenth, the Western Christian powers who undertook the recovery of the Holy Land from the Moslems
further militarized the cross and emphasized Constantine's slogan.
Those who went on these daring military adventures under the sign
of the cross were the Crusaders whose exploits have left their mark
on history, particularly in their contribution to this captivity of the
church. Throughout the intervening centuries the same militarization
of the cross has continued as an almost universal trend in Christen-
dom. Indeed, if any epoch may be selected during which it came
to a climax, the period from 1914 to 1945 would probably be the
one. This was the period within which the two world wars were
fought in which the sword-embossed cross as a military memorial to
those who lost their lives became so prominent. In effect, this meant
that the cross of Christ had been transformed into a symbol of
sacrifice, especially military sacrifice. This meant in turn that its
meaning had been transformed into the very opposite of its New
Testament meaning—where it is a symbol of love signifying that
Christ gave himself for our sins and who out of love, even for those
who crucified him, prayed to his Father that they might be forgiven.

What the militarization of the cross symbolizes is one important
if not the most obvious aspect of the *captivity of the church by
nationalism.* The latter is wider in its range than the former, even
though the former is highly dramatic and most revealing in the
manner in which it has perverted the biblical meaning of the cross.
Therefore, in assessing the captivity of the church by nationalism, it
has to be remembered, as Käsemann says in *Jesus Means Freedom,*
that for more than 1,500 years the churches have normally been on

the side of the ruling classes. There have always been exceptions to this—smaller churches, dissident groups, those calling for reform, pacifists, and the like. But Käsemann is speaking of what has *normally* happened. Indeed, since the rise of the nation states in Western history, with nationalism on the upsurge as a popular ideology and the development of military power through science and technology, the churches on the whole have been even more captivated by nationalism. The outbreak of openly declared warfare usually manifests this very clearly, as the churches of the opposing sides support the war effort, pray for victory, supply chaplains, and see in Christ the servant of the flag and see his cross as the symbol of the sacrifice necessary for victory. In this context the designation of the churches as Christian is subordinated to their designation as Canadian, American, English, Scottish, Irish, French, German, or whatever the particular nation may be. It is the most extreme and radically opposite of anything that could be conceived as valid Christian ecumenism.

The extent to which the church can be captivated by nationalism was well illustrated in Germany the latter part of the nineteenth and the first half of the twentieth century. This involved the infiltration of the church by what was called the Germanic religion or ideology. There was also a fusion of such Germanic religion or ideology with the Christian faith to produce what was essentially patriotic folk mysticism. It had been preceded in the nineteenth century by the fusion of Christianity with German Idealism (quasi-nationalistic) and Romanticism on the part of leading figures in literature, philosophy, theology, and biblical studies. This had led to what was known as *Kulturreligion,* which because of its prestige infiltrated and captivated the church all the more effectively because few recognized at the time what was really happening. But it all became evident with a startling suddenness and ruthlessness when patriotic folk mysticism emerged from the *Kulturreligion* and the Germanic religion or ideology to inspire National Socialism and the rise of Adolf Hitler as the Führer. Out of all of this came the Second World War in its virtually explosive proportions. In such a situation it was tragically apparent how deeply the church, with a few exceptions, was in captivity to German nationalism in a new totalitarian form. Patriotic folk mysticism was the motivating power—the particular form of the Invisible

Religion which had erupted from the depths below.[6,7,8]

Shifting now from Germany to America, it is important to recognize that a similar patriotic folk mysticism developed during the two decades following the Second World War. This was called the "American Religion." It was more or less parallel with the Cold War and implicit in the upsurge of religion which characterized this whole period. Attention was drawn to its nature by a number of studies made of it, the best known of which was probably that of Herberg in his volume *Protestant-Catholic-Jew*.[9] His thesis was that these three religious traditions were being eroded in their particularity and becoming more alike in terms of a fourth religion called the "American Religion." It was infiltrating them and in this respect captivating them by its nationalism. Herberg's research which was done in the early fifties was supported by the research of the Oxford University sociologist Brian Wilson in the mid-sixties.[10] Both pointed in the same direction—the captivity of American Protestantism, Catholicism, and Judaism by nationalism. Where it could have led, if circumstances had ever approached the extremity of those in Germany, is difficult to say. But it was of sufficient similarity to German patriotic folk mysticism to cause a considerable degree of concern among those who were able to recognize its potential. Few were as discerning as Karl Barth in his description of mysticism as esoteric atheism.[11] According to him, open atheism is artless and "blabs out" the secret implicit in mysticism. This would have been shocking to those Americans who during the Cold War saw their upsurge of religion as a protest against atheism. At the same time, perhaps it was the secret atheism of their patriotic folk mysticism which the "Death of God" theologians "blabbed out" in the sixties. But, if anything, they "blabbed it out" too soon, which was probably the reason why their message faded out and in effect was repressed.

There is another captivity of the church to which Gibson Winter, the Chicago sociologist, drew attention at the beginning of the sixties which has implications reaching beyond those evident at the time and which are still highly relevant. This is the kind suggested by the title of his book, *The Suburban Captivity of the Churches*.[12] It presupposes the fact that, during the decades immediately following the Second World War, the suburban areas in America grew at eleven times the rate of the major cities. There was a vast exodus from the cities as well as from other sectors of society of c class of people which became known as the New Middle Class. It was this class which largely populated suburbia. Associated with this exodus was a similar exodus of the churches, so that in the same interval the main line of denominations largely became suburban based. This revealed the highly significant fact of how closely these denominations were associated with the New Middle Class and were supported by it. Out of this fact the conclusion naturally followed that the *suburban captivity of the churches* was largely their captivity to the New Middle Class.[13,14]

But what did this signify? What *was* the New Middle Class? In providing a brief answer to this question, it may be said that the New Middle Class are generally known as knowledge workers. They include professionals, executives, technicians, accountants, teachers, advertisers, and various other types of specialists. What most characterizes this class is that it is chiefly employed by large organizations and especially by companies and corporations. What the captivity to the New Middle Class means is an indirect captivity of the church to large organizations and especially to companies and corporations. The more the individual is converted to his company or corporation as a devotee of the Invisible Religion and at the same time is an active member of a suburban church, the more he pulls or influences his church in the direction of his company. The collective influence of hundreds of thousands, if not millions, of people like him who are more converted to their company than to their church only strengthens this pull or influence of the church in the direction of companies or corporations.

Again, to emphasize the point, the captivity of the New Middle Class implicit in the suburban captivity of the churches is indirectly and subliminally a captivity of the church in general by companies and corporations. In keeping with the Invisible Religion of Corporate Power, it is an invisible captivity. It shapes the political and social outlook, the consciousness and thought of church-going people of this type. It influences their Christian life, work, and worship deeply and subliminally. The reality of the captivity lies beneath the surface. It is never mentioned in the message, teaching, policy, or practice of the church. But let any courageous preacher reveal what Jesus and certain of the apostles and prophets taught concerning the rich and the poor, the oppression of the latter by the former, about the love of money and how hard it is for the rich to enter the kingdom of God, and the reaction would probably be quick and severe. He would probably be accused of preaching "politics," perhaps of a radical kind, and in the end would lose his position. Yet all that he would have done would be the exposition of passages of the Bible and elements in the teaching of Jesus from which they have been protected or had never heard or chosen to read or study.

To this point the captivity of the church to the invisible religion of business and industrial power has been more or less indirect, through the hidden influence of the vocational commitments (conversions?) of its parishioners as members of the New Middle Class. The influence is more contextual, a seldom verbalized ethos which affects everything the church proclaims, teaches, and does through the mode of life and outlook of its parishioners. But nothing has been said as yet of the direct captivity of the church by the business and industrial world. This concerns its actual integration into this world in the literal sense of the term. This, of course, is a relatively new development in the long history of the church and the introduction of a deep and far reaching positive bias in its attitude toward business and industrial power. Concealed within this bias is a positive dedication to the Invisible Religion of Corporate Power.

This integration has already been indicated briefly in chapter two in the discussion of church business and industrial enterprises and large scale investments in the money markets. As also indicated this direct integration is kept relatively secret (and in some cases very secret) so that the average parishioner knows little about it. Church business and industrial enterprises cover a wide range and variety, including the hotel and restaurant business, the food industry, banks and insurance companies, railways and the shipping industry, merchandising and textile and appliance industries, and many other types. In addition are the enormous investments in the money markets of the world which yield a steady flow of income, independent of the offerings of the people. At this point several questions emerge. To what extent is all of this comparable to the money changers whom Jesus drove out of the ancient Jewish Temple—a temple virtually in captivity to the wealthy Sudducaean priestly aristocracy? Or if it be argued that the proceeds of these church industries and investments are used for charitable purposes, to what extent is this the equivalent of a welfare or socialistic state? And finally, what happens when church industries and investments add to the organizational character of the headquarters or head office of the church and transform it more and more into a bureaucracy? Indeed, what happens when its religion is transformed into what may be called "Managerial Religion"?[15]

Coming to another form of captivity which is closely related to and indeed integral to the others, it may be said that the church is in *captivity to the comfort of its privacy.* This arises out of the fact that the New Middle Class do not want any prophets to appear in their pulpits to point out their invisible sin or the error of their idea of justification (salvation) by success. They do not want any preacher or teacher to involve them in the politics of power or more specifically to expose their dedication to the Invisible Religion of Corporate Power. This to them would probably be offensive if not an anathema. So they expect to be comforted, not challenged.[16] They expect to be pleased by a minister, who for this reason has a marketable personality with which they can identify in what is really an idolatrous loyalty, although they do not recognize it as such. At the same time he has to please them to retain his position and therefore obey the hidden, built-in pleasure principle which the method of choice and support of him involves. As one who comforts but does not challenge and who keeps off politics, business, economics, and in general the objective world, his ministry and their religious life are turned inwards upon the subjective. It is privatized and the process and technique by which this is done is called privatization. The result is what the German martyr Bonhoeffer called "cheap grace,"[17] and which has its correlate in what may be called "cheap sin," the meaning of which is at once suggested by the title of a recent, penetrating study of the subject entitled "Whatever Happened to Sin?" (Menninger). A further result of such captivity of the church to the comfort of its privacy is the development of a private enclave in which activities and festivities proliferate along with organizations, all of which are intended to please the people. Services of worship tend to become staged events within the enclave in which the participants are expected to put a good performance, enhanced if desired by color, style, and the aesthetics of robes and liturgy. Needless to say, the primary task of the clergyman is administration, followed by counseling and not that of preaching and teaching, to which he devotes only a relatively small proportion of his time. He becomes a pastor director or more accurately a pastor administrator of managerial religion.

The Historical Perseverance of Biblical Faith

Over against all that has been said to this point on the captivity of the church and the way in which the Judeo-Christian religion in particular has so often yielded to the temptation implicit in the Invisible Religion of Corporate Power, it must now be emphasized that there have always been those who have not yielded to this temptation and the captivity which it brings. They have stood firmly and courageously in their faith, even though it has often involved suffering, persecution, and death. They have exemplified what has become known historically as the perseverance of the saints. They have dared to communicate in their own way and in their own time the central message of the Bible. To mention only a few outstanding examples, there were Elijah, Jeremiah, and Amos among the ancient Hebrews who witnessed in the form of the strongest protest at the risk of their lives. They would not be captivated by the kind of power which denied or repressed their faith and that of their people. Jeremiah in particular could not refrain from speaking out because the message he proclaimed was like a fire burning within his heart and shut up within his bones (Jer. 20:9). He was inwardly compelled to speak. He could not remain silent.

As the one who revealed the most amazing perseverance—a perseverance which led to his death on the cross and his triumph over death—Jesus himself is *normative* of what this really signifies. His perseverance arose out of divine love, involving the divine initiative in searching for the lost, even including his enemies and those whose tyranny over others signified the imposition of various kinds of captivity. Yet Jesus would not bow to any form of captivity but so spoke the truth in love that such truth made men free. For this reason his perseverance may be described at greater length because it inspired so many to follow him in the succeeding centuries and experience liberation in the deepest sense.

His perseverance out of divine love was evident, for example, in his compassion upon the "multitudes" who largely consisted of the "people of the land" or peasants. These included such types as fishermen, donkey drivers, peddlers, prostitutes, and beggars— all of whom as virtually outcastes and untouchables were in a dreadful *captivity to class discrimination* and therefore oppressed. As such they suffered under an inequitable tax system and poverty. Being unable to support the Temple or synagogues, they were generally regarded as irreligious by those higher in the class struc- ture like the Pharisees or Sadducees. Indeed, Jesus as a "carpenter" was considered as one of these at the lowest level in society. Yet he championed their cause, not only in proclaiming his message and identity, but by his actions and teachings in calling upon those who were evidently higher in the social scale to feed the hungry, give drink to the thirsty, clothe the naked, visit the sick, welcome the stranger, and come to those in prison (Matt. 25:35–37). In such an example of the teaching of Jesus, which is similar to the social concern as evidence of valid faith in the Epistle of James (2:1–7, 14–17), Jesus is persevering in his divine love for them. He is not only delivering them from their captivity to class discrimination, especially those who heard his message and responded, but he is delivering them from their sin—including the sin peculiar to their social and economic status.

The perseverance of Jesus in his divine mission of love is further illustrated by his confrontation with the Pharisees in their *captivity to nationalism.* For the most part the Pharisees were a laymen's holiness movement which believed that the stricter their obedience to the mass of complicated tradition which they had added to the Old Testament Law, the sooner God would establish his divine kingdom on earth. For them this would be a Jewish political kingdom and therefore essentially nationalistic. Two of the main areas in which Jesus broke through this tradition were those of Sabbath observance and ceremonial purification. Indeed, the mass of compli- cated tradition consisted of such detailed requirements considered as law—both religious and political—that in order to do good to others, to heal the sick and afflicted for example, that Jesus had to break such law and be considered a law breaker. He could not reveal his love toward others, including the Pharisees, without violating these strict legal minutiae which they considered holy. As one thing led to another, the Pharisees began to despise him and sought to destroy him. They were blind to his love because of their hatred of him implicit in their holiness. They exemplified in their captivity to their nationalism that sin so often seen in religion throughout history: hating within the holy. At the same time the Pharisees were a relatively powerful religious movement which in this era dominated the Sanhedrin, the high court at Jerusalem. Their basic belief in holiness indicated that their obedience to law and tradition as they defined these presupposed a power which they themselves possessed, and which could force God to act more quickly in establishing his nationalistic kingdom on earth.

As Jesus went up to Jerusalem on his last visit to this sacred center of the Judaic religion symbolized by the Temple and its priestly establishment, he was confronted by another captivity which profoundly tested his perseverance in his mission. This was the *captivity of priestly power and wealth* represented by the Sadducean aristocracy which dominated the Temple. This last visit was not solely for the purpose of being crucified as if he had a masochistic death wish, but a mission which arose out of his divine love for his people and even for the Sadducees if in any way he could liberate them from their captivity. The Gospel of John provides more evidence of his ministry in Jerusalem on this last visit, which of course he knew was dangerous and would probably end in his death. But he was fearless in his divine love, with no desire to evade his responsibility by fleeing into the safer regions of Northern Palestine and establishing a church center there which would be pure in faith and doctrine. There was no evidence of such false separatism in Jesus by which he could have avoided the corrupted priestly clique in Jerusalem with their love of power and money. In a short time, of course, the chief priests and their associates stirred up the people against Jesus and were mainly instrumental in having him crucified. In this respect it was high religion which put Jesus to death. It could not recognize genuine divine love, as in him it was manifested in the most unique form.

There was also the *Captivity of Palestine to Roman Power* which was directly imposed through the Procurators and indirectly through the puppet Herodian rulers. The perseverance of Jesus against this captivity is less evident than against the other forms of captivity described to this point. He displayed the same fearless mission of love under this captivity even though he was less frequently confronted by it, except in the end in the Roman trial under Pontius Pilate who condemned him to death by crucifixion. Later in the Book of Acts, as the early church struggled to achieve catholicity in which there would be neither Jew nor Greek, and by implication neither Jew nor Roman, but all one in him irrespective of race, nationality, class, or sex, the spirit of Jesus is reflected. His mission was one of grace alone *(sola gratia)* in which his divine love and that of the Eternal Father who sent him into the world would be the most powerful factor in liberating mankind from all forms of captivity.

A similar perseverance was clearly evident in the life and witness of the apostle Paul as he went from one place to another on his missionary journeys. The constant danger to his life which he experienced is best expressed in his own words "I face death every day" (1 Cor. 15:31, Jerusalem Bible). A similar perseverance was evident in the life and witness of Stephen the martyr, and of Peter, John, Silas, Timothy, and many others in the early church. Indeed, it was evident in the early church as a whole, which in a single generation spread out from Palestine into most of the Graeco-Roman world at a time when transportation and accommodation were primitive compared with modern forms. It was most evident in those periods in the history of the early church when its people refused to worship certain of the emperors of Rome and suffered martyrdom as a result.

Similar examples of martyrdom could be cited throughout the intervening centuries from the ancient past to the present, all revealing the unique perseverance of those who were faithful to the central message of the Bible and their Lord. But it is not necessary to expand upon them except to say that the recent modern world, surprisingly enough, has provided a number of outstanding examples. One of these was Dietrich Bonhoeffer who out of faith in the God of the Bible persevered even though imprisoned and eventually put to death by the Nazis. There have been others like him who suffered a similar fate under the Nazis, Communists, and various tyrannical rulers.

But the necessity of perseverance in biblical faith comes closer to home in our own advanced industrial society, when its Invisible Religion of Corporate Power is seen as a basic threat to the very center of the Judeo-Christian religion. At this point the perseverance of faith concerns the infiltration of the Judeo-Christian religion by the Invisible Religion of Corporate Power—an infiltration as yet so seemingly positive that it virtually deceives the very elect, as the old saying puts it. This means that the crucial problem is the necessity of evangelical liberation and renewal arising out of the perseverance of faith as these involve a deepened and enriched understanding of the gospel—the central message of the Bible.

7.
evangelical liberation and renewal

Evangelical liberation from captivity to the Invisible Religion of Corporate Power involves first the clearest recognition of how such captivity has falsified the gospel under the cover of what seems to be positive religious devotion.[1] It is the clearest recognition of how this kind of positive coverup is common to the themes of chapters two to five: "The Ecumenism of Power," "The Conversion of the Individual," "Justification [salvation] by Success," and "The Invisible Sin." The positive coverup is the aesthetic imagery or idolatry running through these themes and evident in the captivity of the church as developed in chapter six. It is a common factor to them all, especially because of the common emphasis on progress, development, advanced industrialism, new technology, and the style of life which these provide.

In each instance secular power based on bureaucracy, technology, technique, money, and goods and services is the primary objective or consideration and therefore such that it erodes or displaces genuine love *(agape)*, genuine community *(koinonia)*, and genuine personal freedom, truth, and forgiveness as these are depicted in the Bible and the gospel. The subtlety with which it is able to erode and displace these is explained by the positive coverup provided by the aesthetic imagery and idolatry. Everything is made to look and sound so good and proper.

In "The Ecumenism of Power," for example, the unity which comes from bureaucratic power and complexity and promotionalism is made to look so good and proper that one does not see that the unity is not based on genuine love *(agape)* for the personal and genuine community as depicted in the catholicity of the gospel. In "The Conversion of the Individual," the emphasis on his dedication to others in the service of his company or corporation is not out of love for them as in the gospel. Indeed, as a positive form of "slavery" which he usually does not even see himself, it is in principle no different from the service of a robot or an automation to others. In "Justification [salvation] by Success," in which success is considered either as adding credit to the heavenly ledger (meritorious) or as a form of divine favor, the concept is thoroughly false as judged by the meaning of salvation by grace alone in Christ, which is at the heart of the gospel. It is thoroughly man-centered, both from the point of view of the individual and that of the corporate body which employs him. But this, of course, is concealed both by positive imagery and by a superficial, eroded form of the gospel which blends with such imagery. In "The Invisible Sin" it is not merely the more common forms of concealed sin, such as stealing within the law and lying within the truth, but something much more subtle and again positive and seemingly progressive. It is the discontinuity and reductionism with their resultant production of emptiness and how these depersonalize the individual—in biblical terminology, destroy his soul. Again the invisibility is served by positive, aesthetic imagery. It all looks so good, progressive, and efficient. But in the process of depersonalizing thousands upon thousands of individuals to any significant degree, it is destroying their souls and producing what may be described as a lost society—one that does not know where it is, where it is going, or from whence it has come.

All of this emphasizes the importance of a further dimension of evangelical liberation, namely: its heightening of the individual's awareness of his personal esteem and worth which in turn contributes to his perseverance in faith.[2] The basic source of such heightening of personal esteem and worth is the love of God as revealed in the gospel. It is this love of God which in Christ accepts the sinful individual as he is—the love which in the crucified Christ suffered death and triumphed over death for the individual. Thus, whoever the individual may be, to have faith in this God and his divine love is to accept not only God in Christ but himself as one who is precious in the sight of God. Indeed, no other faith ever put such an emphasis on the preciousness of the personal. Therefore because of God's love for him, the individual believer must not only love God and his neighbor but also love himself. Such genuine self love is the very opposite of selfishness. It is an awareness of himself as precious in the sight of God. It is a reverence for himself as belonging to God. As a result this liberates the individual from captivity to loyalties which would depersonalize him and which would possibly lead him to exploit and even kill his neighbor—even such loyalties as those towards a company or corporation, a nation or a flag, a government or military power.

Evangelical liberation therefore involves a further dimension, namely: the creation of genuine community beginning with the community of faith and reaching out to the neighbor who includes the stranger like the wounded man on the road to Jericho whom the Good Samaritan rescued (Luke 10:29–37). Just as the individual comes to know through Christ that he himself is precious in the sight of God, so he comes to know that his fellow believer and his neighbor, including the stranger, is precious in the sight of God. Thus the creation of genuine community, beginning with the community of faith as unique (as those bound together by their love of God for one another and a deep friendly concern for one another), is a liberating influence in a world increasingly populated by urbanized masses who are lonely and generally estranged from one another. [3,4] This is why the church should strive in every way to promote genuine community—that is to say, fellowship or deep friendship among its members and not assume that organizations and activities are the same as such a community. It not infrequently happens that its members have to be liberated from the influence of church organizations and activities in order to come to know one another as friends in the unique sense in which Christ thought of his disciples as friends and not as servants (John 15:15).

This genuine community of faith—signified by the Greek term *koinonia*—is characterized by catholicity in its original meaning as "universal." Perhaps the best definition of such catholicity is found in Paul's Epistle to the Galatians (3:28) where he says that "there is neither Jew nor Greek, there is neither slave nor free, there is neither male nor female; for you are all one in Christ Jesus." This means that in the genuine community of faith there is no place for racial or national discrimination, no place for class discrimination, and no place for sex discrimination. The conclusion is at once obvious that the church in most, if not all, its denominations and branches is in deep need itself of evangelical liberation from these three forms of discrimination. But the conclusion is equally obvious that these three forms of discrimination reflect the influence of the world, the society, and corporate power which has entered into the church and corrupted its understanding of the gospel. So the task of the church is not only the evangelical liberation of itself from these three forms of discrimination, but the evangelical liberation of the world, the society, and corporate power around it as well.

It follows, therefore, that one of the important tasks of the church is that of learning to know in depth and accuracy the society and world in which it lives and proclaims the gospel. This is not easy because of the extent to which corporate power and complex urban society operates in the realm of secrecy. But it is vital to the work of the church and evangelical liberation. If one knows the Bible and nothing but the Bible, one does not know the Bible. Similarly, if one knows the gospel and nothing but the gospel, one does not know the gospel. Indeed, the gospel obligates the church to know the society and world around it in order to understand the situation and context into which its preaching and teaching are orientated. This was certainly true of Jesus as reflected in his parables, which in most instances were pictures of the contemporary world around him— situations rather than texts from the Old Testament which he used to proclaim his message. In other words, in his parables Jesus often used the contextual form instead of the textual and therefore spoke out of a particular situation. This obviously required a knowledge in depth and accuracy of the society and world in which he lived. This was one of the reasons why the message of Jesus was so liberating and at the same time one of the reasons why it was dangerous for him.

This same need applies to the church. If it is to persevere and proclaim the gospel in such a way as to remind the society and world around it (and especially corporate power) of their social obligations based on justice, genuine concern, and love, it must have this depth and accuracy of knowledge. It must really know, for example, the local and multi-national operations of corporate power in order to make an effective evangelical witness. The gospel has a social as well as a personal dimension, as evident not only in the life, teaching, and preaching of Jesus, but in the testimony of his apostles (e.g. James 2:1–7, 14–17; 5:1–6). This social dimension is not what has been commonly known as the "social gospel," but it is evidence in social action of the validity of the personal dimension of the gospel which has been accepted and believed. As such it is never easy, as Jesus knew in his challenging of the various forms of corporate power in his day. It involves the kind of perseverance which he, his Apostles, and the early church and its saints exemplified throughout the ages.

Coming now to the question of what is involved in evangelical renewal which all evangelical liberation presupposes, perhaps it is best to begin with theological education in the seminaries and colleges and with Christian education in the churches. The question in both areas of education, and more surprisingly in theological education, is the extent to which a student may complete his undergraduate program and indeed an advanced degree program and at the end not really know what the gospel means. In raising this question the concern involves the meaning of the gospel in its richness of depth and multidimensional form as the core message of the Bible which runs from the beginning to the end—from Genesis to Revelation.[5]

Insofar as this question is valid, certain observations can be made. The *first* is that the core curriculum should be designed to deepen the students' understanding and faith in this core message of the Bible. It should focus on this core message so that, no matter whether the student be enrolled in a seminary or college or in a church school, this will be the central theme of his education. The *second* observation is that any electives or specialties taken by him should bear a substantial and enriching relationship to this core message. They should not distract from it or be in any sense irrelevant to it so that the student becomes absorbed by them and the orientation of his education becomes distorted. In other words, his theological or church school education should be characterized by evangelical coordination. A *third* observation should be briefly made at this point even though it repeats what has been already stated earlier. It concerns the emphasis on an adequate and accurate knowledge of the society and world in which the student lives. Even though he knows the gospel in its depth and richness of meaning, he will not really know what the gospel means if he does not know the world around him in a similar depth, along with its poverty of spirit and bondage to sin and death. This knowledge of the world around him should also be characterized by evangelical coordination. It should be relevant to the gospel.

In order to signify what evangelical renewal involves, it seems appropriate to provide a series of observations which may be helpful in their collective impression of suggesting what the gospel means. These are provided as concluding observations of a positive nature—as guidelines to further reflection on evangelical renewal. They are listed in numerical sequence and condensed in style and substance.

(1) The gospel is good news—the best news that anyone can hear—joyful news—truth that is stranger than fiction.

(2) The gospel is good news in a world where most news is bad news—fires, floods, storms, accidents, robberies, murders, riots, revolutions, wars, and deaths—which though sensational and sales-worthy signify hopelessness.

(3) The gospel is good news not in the relative sense of a good medical, financial, or academic report which may change tomorrow. It is good news in the absolute sense like a report that is final, to which nothing can be added or taken away—a report that stands —that is permanent and ultimate.

(4) The gospel does not grow old in a single day—like the daily news—only to be discarded and forgotten. It is the good news which, though old in time, is always becoming new. To hear it once inspires the wish to hear it again like a little child who never tires of its favorite story and repeatedly exclaims, "Daddy (Abba), tell it again."

(5) The gospel is heard at the point where all human resources have reached their limit; where medical, legal, and financial assistance fail; where sociology, psychology, and counseling have nothing more to say; where there are no longer human answers and solutions. This is where the work of the minister of the gospel really begins—a work which is more difficult for him if he imagines he should have the answer for every question and the technique for every situation. For his work to become effective he must blend his voice with that of the prophet Habakkuk and accept the absurdity so often found in life: "Though the fig tree do not blossom, nor fruit be on the vines, the produce of the olive fail and the fields yield no food, the flock be cut off from the fold and there be no herd in the stalls, yet I will rejoice in the Lord I will joy in the God of my salvation" (Hab. 3:17–18).

(6) The gospel transforms basic motivation—the basic reason why we live, why we do what we do, why we get up in the morning and go to work and why we think our work has genuine significance. The gospel is therefore not heard if only with the ear and not with the mind; if only with the mind and not with the heart; if only on the surface of life and not in the depths where basic motivation is functioning.

(7) The gospel is simple and yet profound; so simple a child can understand it, so profound that the most learned ones can never fathom it. It is the message of genuine love, holy love—a love that is never fathomed by ordinary love and least of all by love expressed as erotic desire. Therefore we must not falsify its simplicity into the superficial, nor its profundity into intellectuality, nor its message of genuine, holy love merely into an appeal to feeling and subjectivity.

(8) Good people need to hear the gospel as much as bad people, successful people as much as failures, misfits, and derelicts; the mentally healthy, happy and well integrated as much as the neurotic, insane, and broken people. All have the same basic problems in common. They all sin and have to die.

(9) In its simplest form the gospel means that God in Christ is for us and not against us. This is the confidence reflected in the testi-

mony of the apostle Paul: "If God be for us, who can be against us?" (Rom. 8:31, KJV). The importance of this confidence arises out of the fact that individually and collectively we are most often against ourselves. Indeed, Menninger's *Man Against Himself* [6] is the sad commentary which may be written over human history. Therefore, God for us and not against us means that God protects us from ourselves, especially when we are divided against ourselves individually and collectively.

(10) The gospel therefore reminds us of how precious each person is in the sight of God regardless of race, nationality, sex, class, or creed; religious or irreligious; atheistic or Christian; violent or law-abiding. It therefore warns against the tyranny of self-judgment, whether this be expressed as self-conceit or self-condemnation. Again this concerns God's protection of ourselves *from* ourselves out of the eternal love which in Christ he has shown towards us.

(11) The gospel is the message (revelation) of reconciliation. The urgency of hearing it is indicated by the amount of conflict in the world—racial, national, class, and sex; political, economic, and social; familial, marital, and sibling, as well as intra-psychical and unconscious. Such conflict explodes from time to time into argument and violence with a legacy of broken hearts and homes—of hatred and disillusionment.

(12) The gospel of reconciliation does not mean the elimination of all conflict, as if all forms of conflict were bad. The elimination of the conflict of life against death can mean the elimination of life in favor of death. This is why the desire to avoid conflicts at any price—to be passive, silent, and always peaceful—can result in dead churches and dead people even though seemingly alive. It is reconciliation with death.

(13) Therefore, the gospel of reconciliation does not mean reconciliation with nothingness (vacuity, emptiness). It is not the resignation to the conviction that we came from nothingness and will return to nothingness and that we live and move and have our being in nothingness. It is not in this sense the reconciliation with darkness.[7]

(14) Instead, the reconciliation is distinguished by its ultimate, loving concern for the personal based upon the conviction that the ultimate (God)—which is anterior to all existence, all forms of being —is personal and the final definition of the mystery of the personal.

(15) In this context and in light of what has been said previously, the gospel of reconciliation is concerned with what may be called the divine triangle, namely: reconciliation with God, with one's neighbor, and with oneself. Each type of reconciliation presupposes and involves the others. Reconciliation with God is the primary type symbolized by the apex of the triangle upon which the validity and reality of the other two types depend.

(16) Reconciliation with God does not mean reconciliation with him as if he were one object among other objects but rather to him as one who is personally "objective" in the sense of his "otherness" (transcendence). It is reconciliation with him as the all-embracive God, whose loving power comprehends and maintains the existence of all things, including oneself and one's neighbor. To be reconciled to him as one object among other objects would transform him into an idol just as it would one's neighbor and oneself.

(17) The essence of sin for which reconciliation to God is the indispensable remedy is only evident at the point where all conventional sins lose their significance. This is the point at which the enigma of man's destructiveness, his hardness of heart, his role as a killer, his deceit, greed, exploitation, idolatry, nihilism, and darkness deep within himself defy definition. This is the point of the mystery of ultimate negation which in essence means his hatred of God.

(18) There are three principal forms of hatred of God depending upon the direction in which the hatred is expressed. If the hatred is directed towards him it results in the denial of him. If it is directed away from him it results in the desire to escape from him. If it is directed neither towards nor away from him in what amounts to a positional neutrality, it results in indifference. All of these forms— denial, escape, and indifference are forms of hatred, each of which is a form of atheism.

(19) Such hatred of God in these three forms, which are inevitably expressed toward the neighbor and the self (triangular), generate guilt. Such guilt is "objective" guilt, which means "objective" with respective to time. The deed, thought, or motive which incurs guilt recedes into the past and cannot be brought back again to be undone or rectified. Because the individual is not free to change his past—a past which nevertheless conditions his present—he is no longer free with respect to his deed. His guilt signifies a bondage. In this respect it is a bondage which his freedom of will is unable to overcome. This arouses further hatred in the same tri-dimensional form—which in turn produces more guilt. As the vicious circle enlarges, the bondage increases and tends toward deadness—a hardening, as it were, of the heart.

(20) Finally, it should be emphasized that reconciliation through the life and death of Christ, which is the revelation of God's love for man in his bondage to "objective" guilt and therefore the forgiveness of sin, is not of itself the complete gospel. The power of the resurrection is integral to such forgiveness, indeed its fulfilment, as Easter comes into the heart of man. This Easter power of love is primarily the transcendent presence of the Holy Spirit of Christ and the Father in the heart of man which transforms him. It gives him a unique and sustaining hope in the realization that the best is yet before him—that there is nothing to fear. To use a Pauline metaphor, it means pressing toward the mark, like a Greek runner sprinting at the end of the race to reach the finishing line more quickly—the mark being the upward calling of God, including all that is meant by the Christian hope which involves the Second Advent. It is not a hope for believers only as individuals but also for the church and the whole world—the whole creation. If the beginning of all things (their creation) is good news, the end of all things (their destiny) is good news.

notes

Chapter 1

1. Hannah Arendt, *The Origins of Totalitarianism* (Cleveland and New York: Meridian Books, World Publishing Co., 2nd ed. 1958), p. 403.
2. W.I. Thompson, *The Edge of History* (New York: Harper & Row, 1971). See p. 49 re. shift toward behavioral sciences at M.I.T.
3. Bertrand de Jouvenal, "Intellectuals and Power," *Center Magazine* (Center for the Study of Democratic Institutions, Santa Barbara, California), Jan.-Feb. 1973, pp. 51–56.
4. As an example of an extra-biblical apocalypse, *The Apocalypse of Baruch,* ed. R.H. Charles (London: Adam and Charles Black, 1896), provides an emphatic example of abundance. In ch. 29, the apocalyptic grapevine would yield 120 billion gallons of wine.
5. Robert Theobald, ed., *Dialogue on Technology* (New York: Bobbs-Merrill Co., 1967), pp. 23–24, 73–80.
6. Lewis Mumford, *The Pentagon of Power* (New York: Harcourt Brace Jovanovich, 1970). Graphic Section I:10.
7. Dennis Gabor, *Inventing the Future* (New York: Alfred A. Knopf, 1963).
8. C.S. Lewis, *The Abolition of Man* (Riddell Memorial Lectures, 1943, Oxford University Press, 1944), p. 28.
9. Andrew Hacker, *The End of the American Era* (New York: Atheneum, 1970; Toronto: McLelland and Stewart, 1970). See also re. overclass and underclass in Gibson Winter, *Being Free* (New York: Macmillan, 1970; Toronto: Collier-MacMillan, 1970).
10. Frank Milligan (Associate Director for University Affairs, Canada Council), "The Universities: Present Perplexities and Future

Needs" (Address in Montreal, April 5, 1976; Ottawa: The Canda Council.)

11. Ernst Käsemann, *Jesus Means Freedom* (Philadelphia: Fortress Press, 1970), p. 137.

12. Thomas Luckmann, *The Invisible Religion* (New York: Macmillan, 1967).

13. Martin Esslin, *The Theatre of the Absurd* (Garden City, N.Y.: Anchor Books, Doubleday & Co., 1961), pp. 42–45, 297–99.

14. T.S. Eliot, *Collected Poems, 1909–1935* (London: Faber & Faber, 1936, 1951), p. 157, "Choruses from the Rock," Part I.

Chapter 2

1. Max Weber, *The Protestant Ethic and the Spirit of Capitalism* (New York: Charles Scribner's Sons, 1930, 1958). Weber's theory, which of course has its limitations and weaknesses, was based upon the relation between the older, individualistic (entrepreneurial) form of Capitalism in relation to the so-called Protestant (work) Ethic. The reference here is to suggest that the theory could be revised to show a relation between the newer monopolistic corporation Capitalism and the ecumenical trend in the churches with its social ethic.

2. Michael Kidron, *Western Capitalism Since the War* (Middlesex, England and Baltimore: Pelican Book published by Penguin Books, Ltd., rev. ed. 1970), pp. 105–110.

3. Mitchell Gordon, *Sick Cities: Psychology and Pathology of American Urban Life* (Baltimore: Penguin Books, 1966). See p. 16 which states that in the decade of the 1960s suburban populations increased 56 percent while the nation's largest cities rose less than 5 percent. Suburbia increased at least 11 times the percentage of these cities.

4. Bryan R. Wilson, *Religion in Secular Society* (Middlesex, England and Baltimore: Pelican Book published by Penguin Books, 1969). See chapters 8, 9, 10.

5. Peter Berger, "The Market Model for the Analysis of Ecumenicity," *Social Research,* vol. 30, 1963, pp. 77–93.

6. Although church wealth and business are played down and kept secret in different ways, especially by the Roman Catholic

Church, the following selected references will at least give some conception of their variety and scope:

M.A. Larson, *Church Wealth and Business Income* (New York: Philisophical Library, 1965); Corrado Pallenburg, *Vatican Finances* (Middlesex, England: Pelican Book by Penguin Books, 1971); Nino LoBello, *The Vatican Empire* (New York and Richmond Hill, Canada: Pocket Books division of Simon & Schuster, 1969); "Should We Tax Our Churches?" in *Look* Magazine, May 19, 1970 (a rather revealing article); *Time* Magazine, November 28, 1969; *Reader's Digest,* March 1969.

7. Gibson Winter, *Religious Identity* (New York and London: Macmillan, 1968). See especially pp. 1–46 re. increased ratio of headquarter staff to church membership (especially Appendix B), agency domination, managerial personnel, etc. See also P.M. Harrison, *Authority and Power in the Free Church Tradition* (Princeton: Princeton University Press, 1959).

8. Ernst Käsemann, *Jesus Means Freedom* (Philadelphia: Fortress Press, 1970), pp. 90, 96–100.

9. Samuel Blizzard, "The Minister's Dilemma," *Christian Century,* April 25, 1956.

10. Winter, *Religious Identity.* This quotation taken from the back cover of the book has been attributed to Winter; it may be instead an editorial comment on the main theme.

11. Ferdinand Lundberg, *The Rich and the Super-Rich* (New York and Toronto: Bantam Books, 1969). See pp. 298–300, Merger Movement.

12. L.T. Morgan (Associate Professor, Political Economy, Univ. of Toronto), *Fascism: From Origins to Maturity in Theory and Practice* (Toronto: Thistle Printing Co., 1942).

13. Andrew Hacker, *The Corporation Take-Over* (Garden City, N.Y.: Anchor Books, Doubleday & Co., 1964), p. 1.

14. Dennis Yates, "Multinational Corporations: A Challenge to the Concept of National Sovereignty," *Andover Newton Quarterly,* vol. 13, no. 3, Jan. 1973, pp. 234–39. See also K. Levitt, *Silent Surrender* (Toronto: MacMillan of Canada, 1970), pp. 92–115 re. "Challenge to the Nation State."

The literature on multi-national corporations is large and increasing. Only a few suggestions can be made here in addition

to references 2, 11–15, and 22, namely: C.R. Mills, *The Power Elite* (Oxford University Press, Galaxy Book, 1959); G.W. Domhoff, *Who Rules America?* (Englewood Cliffs, N.J.: Prentice-Hall, 1967); R. Heilbroner, "Review of Four Books on Multinationals" (*N.Y. Review of Books,* March 20, 1975), pp. 6–10.
15. Lundberg, p. 304.
16. Bertrand de Jouvenal, "Intellectuals and Power," *Center Magazine,* Jan.-Feb. 1973, p. 52.
17. See David Roberts' contribution in *What the Christian Hopes for in Society,* ed. Reinhold Niebuhr (New York: Association Press, 1957), pp. 75–76.
18. John Kenneth Galbraith, *The New Industrial State* (Boston: Houghton Mifflin Co., 1967).
19. Daniel S. Snowman, *America Since 1920* (New York: Harper & Row, 1969). See p. 116 where it is stated that American federal government expenditure during the five years of the Second World War (1941–1945 inclusive) was more than that of the whole of previous American history.
20. Lundberg. See p. 5 for quotation of Eisenhower's warning on the Military-Industrial Complex. For his warning on the scientific technological elite see Ralph Lapp, *The Weapons Culture* (Baltimore: Penguin Books, 1969), p. 17.
21. Galbraith, p. 314.
22. Gabriel Kolko, *The Roots of American Foreign Policy* (Boston: Beacon Press, 1969). See also David Horowitz, ed., *Corporations and the Cold War* (New York: Bertrand Russell Peace Foundation, Monthly Review Press, 1969).
23. Lapp. See Appendix VI and VII for list of colleges, universities, and institutes of technology.
24. John Kenneth Galbraith, *How to Control the Military* (New York: Doubleday, 1969, and Signet Books, New American Library, 1969).
25. Kolko. See re. depletion of resources.
26. References regarding militarism and military power are numerous. The following are merely a few selected titles: F.J. Cook, *The Warfare State* (New York: Macmillan, 1964); Tristram Coffin, *The Armed Society* (Baltimore: Pelican Book by Penguin Books, 1964); Ralph Lapp, *The Weapons Culture* (cited previ-

ously); George Thayer, *The War Business* (New York: Simon & Schuster, 1969, and Discus Books, pub. by Avon, 1970).

27. Yates, pp. 234–39.
28. Jacques Ellul, *The Technological Society* (New York: Alfred A. Knopf, 1964), trans. John Wilkinson. See p. ix, translator's introduction: Ernst Junger once wrote that "technology is the real metaphysics of the twentieth century." See also p. 418 where Ellul speaks of "the real religion of our times," by which means, as he says, "the dominant forces of the technological society."
29. George Orwell, *Nineteen Eighty-Four* (New York: Signet Classic, 1964).
30. David Riesman et al., *The Lonely Crowd* (New Haven: Yale University Press, 1950).
31. Søren Kierkegaard, *Journals* (New York, Toronto, and London: Oxford University Press, 1938), p. 180, section 616.
32. *Ibid.*, section 617.

Chapter 3

1. David Riesman et al., *The Lonely Crowd* (New Haven: Yale University Press, 1950).
2. W.H. Whyte, Jr., *The Organization Man* (Garden City, N.Y.: Anchor Books, Doubleday & Co., 1956).
3. Robert V. Presthus, *The Organizational Society* (New York: Caravelle edition of Vintage Books, Random House, 1962), p. 79. See also chapter 3.
4. Lewis Mumford, *The Pentagon of Power* (New York: Harcourt Brace Jovanovich, 1970), pp. 150–51, 238–40.
5. Eric Hoffer, *The True Believer* (New York: Harper & Row, 1951), pp. 64–65.
6. Marshall McLuhan, *Understanding Media* (New York: Signet Books; Toronto: New American Library of Canada, 1966). See re. concept of implosion.
7. Vance Packard, *The Hidden Persuaders* (New York: David McKay, 1957; in paperback by Pocket Books and in Canada by Pocket Books of Canada, Montreal, 1962.)
8. Erich Fromm, *Escape from Freedom* (New York and Toronto: Farrar and Rinehart, 1941), pp. 119–20.

9. Douglas McGregor, *The Human Side of Enterprise* (New York: McGraw-Hill, 1960). See *Saturday Night,* July 1973, p. 36.
10. Andrew Hacker, *The Corporation Take-Over* (Garden City, N.Y.: Anchor Books, Doubleday & Co., 1964), p. 252.
11. Alan Harrington, "Life in the Crystal Palace," a chapter in Eric and Mary Josephson, eds., *Man Alone* (New York: Dell, 1962), pp. 133–143.
12. F. Dostoevsky, *The Brothers Karamazov* (New York: Signet Classic, New American Library, 4th printing 1954), p. 234.
13. Gunnar Myrdal, *Challenge to Affluence* (New York and Toronto: Vintage Books, Random House, 1965), pp. 44–45.
14. Hacker, p. 13.
15. *Ibid.,* pp. 260–61.
16. Hannah Arendt, *The Origins of Totalitarianism* (Cleveland and New York: Meridian Books, World Publishing Co., 2nd ed. 1958), pp. 156–57.
17. Kressman Taylor, *Until That Day* (New York: Eagle Book, distributed by Duell, Sloan & Pearce, 2nd printing 1942). On pp. 60–63 the author tells of a young German who was converted to Hitler and confessed that he believed and was saved by this new Savior. The book was widely read during the war because it told of experiences under the Nazi regime.
18. Fritz Stern, *The Politics of Cultural Despair: A Study in the Rise of the Germanic Ideology* (Garden City, N.Y.: Anchor Books, Doubleday & Co., 1965). This is a study of the developments in the nineteenth and early twentieth centuries which led to German Nazism. It is of particular interest in that one of the precursors of Nazism (Lagarde, born 1827) invoked the old Christian doctrine of rebirth (*Wiedergeburt,* born again) so central to Pietism and gave it a mystical political meaning pertaining to the rebirth of the nation. By the 1920s this idea had become prominent as political propaganda in many quarters.

Chapter 4

1. Richard Hofstadter, *Anti-Intellectualism in American Life* (New York: Alfred A. Knopf, 1963, and Vintage Books, Random House). See Chapter X, "Self Help and Spiritual Technology" (success-motivated religion).

2. Louis Schneider and Sanford M. Dornbusch, *Popular Religion: Inspirational Books in America* (Chicago: Univ. of Chicago Press, 1958). Surveys the best-selling religious books over an 80-year period (1875–1955). The trend is towards health, happiness, and prosperity. Emphasis is on religion bringing wealth and success as basic to such religion.

3. Martin E. Marty, *The New Shape of American Religion* (New York: Harper, 1959). See especially chapter 2, "The God of Religion in General"; chapter 4, "American Real Religion: An Attitude."

4. John Kenneth Galbraith, *The Affluent Society* (New York: Mentor Book pub. by the New American Library; reprint from hardcover pub. by Houghton Mifflin Co., 1958).

5. Vance Packard, *The Hidden Persuaders* (New York: David McKay, 1957; in paperback by Pocket Books). See in index re. consumer motivation and motivational research.

6. Jules Henry, *Culture Against Man* (New York: Random House, 1963; Vintage Books, 1965). See in index re. consumers and consumption.

7. Theodore Roszak, *The Making of a Counter Culture* (Garden City, N.Y.: Anchor Books, Doubleday & Co., 1969), p. 216.

8. J.J. Servan-Schreiber, *The American Challenge* (New York: Avon Books, English translation 1968, 1969). See p. 79 re. innovation, research, and development as related to competitive production (quantification).

9. William Sargant, *The Battle for the Mind* (London: Pan Books Ltd., revised ed. 1959). See especially chapters 5, 6, 7 pertaining to religion.

10. Tomas G. Masaryk, *Modern Man and Religion* (London: George Allan and Unwin, 1938). See pp. 301–10 re. Wagner and his radical conception of beauty and musical mysticism.

Chapter 5

1. F. Dostoevsky, *The Brothers Karamazov* (New York: Signet Classic, New American Library, 4th printing 1954), p. 234f.

2. Peter F. Drucker, *The Age of Discontinuity* (New York: Harper & Row, 1969).

3. Henry M. Ruitenbeek, *The Individual and the Crowd: A Study of Identity in America* (New York and Toronto: Mentor Book pub. by New American Library, 1965). See pp. 96, 133 re. discontinuity.

4. Marshall McLuhan, *Understanding Media* (New York: Signet Books, New American Library, 1971; Toronto: New American Library of Canada, 1966). See re. concept of implosion, pp. 19–20.

5. Gunther Anders, "Reflections on the H Bomb." See chapter 5, pp. 288–98, in Eric and Mary Josephson, eds., *Man Alone* (New York: Dell, Laurel Edition, 1962).

6. R.H. Charles, ed., *The Apocalypse of Baruch* (London: Adam and Charles Black, 1896). See reference 4 in chapter one of this volume.

7. Lewis Mumford, *The Pentagon of Power* (New York: Harcourt Brace Jovanovich, 1964), pp. 278–79. See in index re. reductionism.

8. Theodore Roszak, *Where the Wasteland Ends* (Garden City, N.Y.: Doubleday & Co., 1972). See chapter 7 and appendix to it on reductionism.

9. T.S. Eliot, *Collected Poems, 1909–1935* (London: Faber & Faber, 1936, 1951). See p. 85, "The Hollow Men."

10. C.S. Lewis, *The Abolition of Man* (Riddell Memorial Lectures, 1943, Oxford University Press, 1944).

11. Wylie Sypher, *Loss of the Self in Modern Literature and Art* (New York: Vintage Books, Random House, 1962). Sypher maintains that, despite various degrees of loss of self, a minimal identity always remains.

12. Martin Esslin, *The Theatre of the Absurd* (Garden City, N.Y.: Anchor Books, Doubleday & Co., 1961). See chapter 1: Samuel Beckett, "The Search for the Self."

13. Henrik Ibsen, *Brand: A Dramatic Poem* (London and Toronto: Everyman's Library, J.M. Dent & Sons; New York: E.P. Dutton & Co., 1917). See pp. 25–26: how everyone has learned to be a little bit of everything.

14. Maurice S. Friedman, *To Deny Our Nothingness* (New York: Delta Book pub. by Dell, 1967).

15. Jean-Paul Sartre, *Being and Nothingness* (New York: Philosophical Library, 1956).
16. Tomas G. Masaryk, *Modern Man and Religion* (London: George Allen and Unwin, 1938).
17. William Barrett, *The Irrational Man* (Garden City, N.Y.: Anchor Books, Doubleday & Co., 1958). See pp. 23–41, "Encounter with Nothingness."
18. Albert Camus, *The Plague* (Middlesex, England: Penguin Books, English trans. 1948).
19. Hermann Rauschning, *The Beast Out of the Abyss* (London, Toronto: William Heinemann Ltd., trans. by E.W. Dickes, 1941). See also his volume, *Germany's Revolution of Nihilism.*
20. Of the earlier studies on the theme of alienation (anomie), those of Durkheim should be consulted; on nothingness (nihilism) and the Antichrist, those of Nietzsche.

Chapter 6

1. N.G. Demerath, *Social Class in American Protestantism* (Chicago: Rand McNally, 1963).
2. Liston Pope, "Religion and the Class Structure," in Reinhard Bendix and Seymour M. Lipset, eds., *Class, Status and Power* (New York: Free Press, 1966), pp. 316–23; *Annals of the American Academy of Political Science,* vol. 256, 1948.
3. Harvey Cox, *The Secular City* (New York: Macmillan, 1965). See creation as the disenchantment of nature; also de-sacralization.
4. Williston Walker, *A History of the Christian Church* (Edinburgh: T. & T. Clark, 1930). See: Constantine I, Emperor of the Crusades.
5. Ethelbert Stauffer, *Christ and the Caesars* (London: S.C.M. Press, 1955). See: Constantine I.
6. Fritz Stern, *The Politics of Cultural Despair: A Study in the Rise of the Germanic Ideology* (Garden City, N.Y.: Anchor Books, Doubleday & Co., 1965).
7. Sydney Dark and R.S. Essex, *The War Against God* (London: Hodder & Stoughton, 1937).
8. Tomas G. Masaryk, *Modern Man and Religion* (London:

George Allen and Unwin, 1938; translated and revised by Kennedy).

9. Will Herberg, *Protestant-Catholic-Jew* (Garden City, N.Y.: Doubleday & Co., 1955).

10. Bryan R. Wilson, *Religion in Secular Society* (Middlesex, England and Baltimore: Pelican Book published by Penguin Books, 1969).

11. Karl Barth, *Church Dogmatics* (Edinburgh: T. & T. Clark, 1936; translation by G.T. Thomson), vol. I, part 3, pp. 318–25.

12. Gibson Winter, *The Suburban Captivity of the Churches* (Garden City, N.Y.: Doubleday & Co., 1961).

13. Andrew Hacker, *The End of the American Era* (New York: Atheneum, 1970; Toronto: McLelland and Stewart, 1970). See New Middle Class, pp. 28–37, 48–51.

14. Andrew Hacker, *The Corporation Take-Over* (Garden City, N.Y.: Anchor Books, Doubleday & Co., 1964). See New Middle Class, pp. 242–43, and following sections.

15. Gibson Winter, *Religious Identity* (New York: Macmillan, 1968).

16. C.Y. Glock, R.B. Ringer, and E.R. Babbie, *To Comfort and Challenge* (Berkeley: Univ. of California Press, 1969).

17. Dietrich Bonhoeffer, *The Cost of Discipleship* (London: S.C.M. Press, 1948, trans. by R.H. Fuller). See chapter 1, "Costly Grace" (pp. 37–49). See reference in this chapter to cheap grace.

Chapter 7

1. Ernst Käsemann, *Jesus Means Freedom* (Philadelphia: Fortress Press, 1970).

2. Henry M. Ruitenbeek, *The Individual and the Crowd: A Study of Identity in America* (New York: Mentor Book pub. by New American Library, 1965). This study emphasizes that the erosion of self-identity is a central problem in American society.

3. David Riesman et al., *The Lonely Crowd* (New Haven: Yale University Press, 1950).

4. Mitchell Gordon, *Sick Cities: Psychology and Pathology of American Urban Life* (Baltimore: Penguin Books, 1965). This volume and that of Riesman are examples of an increasing

literature on these respective themes in our world today.

5. Joachim Jeremias, *The Central Message of the New Testament* (New York: Charles Scribner's Sons, 1965). This is only one example of a large literature on the core message of the New and Old Testaments.

6. Karl A. Menninger, *Man Against Himself* (New York: Harcourt, Brace & Co., 1938).

7. The literature of *nothingness* is also large, including such authors as Nietzsche, Masaryk, Rauschning, and Sartre.